THE CRISIS OF
WESTERN EDUCATION

by CHRISTOPHER DAWSON

With Specific Programs for the
Study of Christian Culture
by JOHN J. MULLOY

SHEED AND WARD—NEW YORK

CONTENTS

PART THREE: WESTERN MAN AND THE TECHNOLOGICAL ORDER

ACKNOWLEDGMENTS

Grateful acknowledgment is made to the editors of *America, The Commonweal, The Critic,* and *Jubilee* for permission to use here material which first appeared in their pages.

THE CRISIS OF
WESTERN EDUCATION

PART ONE

THE HISTORY OF LIBERAL EDUCATION IN THE WEST

I. THE ORIGINS OF THE WESTERN TRADITION OF EDUCATION

Culture, as its name denotes, is an artificial product. It is like a city that has been built up laboriously by the work of successive generations, not a jungle which has grown up spontaneously by the blind pressure of natural forces. It is the essence of culture that it is communicated and acquired, and although it is inherited by one generation from another, it is a social not a biological inheritance, a tradition of learning, an accumulated capital of knowledge and a community of "folkways" into which the individual has to be initiated.

Hence it is clear that culture is inseparable from education, since education in the widest sense of the word is what the anthropologists term "enculturation," i.e., the process by which culture is handed on by the society and acquired by the individual. No doubt this is a far wider process than what is commonly known as education, for we apply the word "education" only to a very specialized type of enculturation—the formal teaching of particular kinds of knowledge and behavior to the younger members of the community through particular institutions. And the most important of all the processes by which culture is transmitted—the acquisition of speech—takes place before formal education begins.

In the past education was an exceptional privilege which was confined to the ruling elements of society, especially the priesthood, and it is only during the last two centuries that any attempt has been made to extend it to the whole society. But it would be a mistake to suppose that in the past the common man was completely uneducated. He was no less "enculturated" than modern man, but he acquired his culture orally and practically by tradition and folklore, by craftmanship and apprenticeship, and through religion and art. Even among primitive peoples this "enculturation" is quite a conscious systematic process, and the youth is initiated into the life and traditions of the tribe by a regular system of training and instruction which finds its climax in the initiation rites.

Such systems may occasionally produce quite an elaborate form of oral education, as in West Africa and still more in Polynesia, but it is only in literate and civilized societies, beginning with those of ancient Sumeria and Egypt, that education in the modern specialized sense became a necessary function in the life of society. The temple schools of ancient Sumer were the seeds of that tree of knowledge which has grown with civilization until it has filled the world. But even in its first beginnings it already possessed many of the characteristics that distinguish the scholar, the scientist and the man of learning. Owing to the difficulty of the original hieroglyphic scripts and their close association with the temple service, the literate class was from the first a privileged minority which tended to become an exclusive corporation. It was not necessarily the ruling class, and it might even be different from the latter in race and language, as seems to have been the case in Babylonia under the Kassites, and thus it involved the possibility of a cleavage or dualism of culture which had important sociological consequences. Nevertheless it possessed an immense prestige as the guardian of the sacred tradition on which the very existence of the civilization depended.

The most remarkable example of this is to be seen in China, where there has been an unbroken tradition of education and scholarship that has continued for thousands of years almost to our own times. Here the Confucian scholars were not merely the guardians of a classical tradition, they were the cement that held Chinese society together. Again and again China was invaded and conquered by the barbarians, and on each occasion the conquerors were eventually obliged to use the services of the scholars without whom the administration of the empire could not be carried on. Before long the servants became the teachers of the conquerors, and the latter were proud to take their appointed place in the ordered hierarchy of the Chinese society.

The case of China is an exceptionally clear example of the way in which the survival of a civilization is dependent on the continuity of its educational tradition. But a similar relation is to be found in every advanced culture. A common educational tradition creates a common world of thought with common moral and intellectual values and a common inheritance of knowledge, and these are the conditions which make a culture conscious of its identity and give it a common memory and a common past. Consequently any break in the continuity of the educational tradition involves a corresponding break in the continuity of the culture. If the break were a complete one, it would be far more revolutionary than any political or economic change, since it would mean the death of the civilization, as has happened apparently in the case of the Maya civilization of Central America.

No doubt it is easier to realize this in civilizations remote from our own, especially in those like China and India where the learned class has become a caste or order set apart from the rest of society. When education has become universal, and reading and writing are no longer regarded as a mystery reserved for a privileged minority, we are apt to forget how recent these conditions are and how strong has been the influence of tradition on Western education. Yet the tradition of liberal education in Western culture is practically as old as the Confucian tradition in China and has played a similar part in forming the mind and maintaining the continuity of our civilization. For the system of classical studies or "humane letters," which still dominated the English universities and public schools when I was young, had its origins some twenty-four centuries ago in ancient Athens and was handed down intact from the Greek sophists to the Latin rhetoricians and grammarians and from these to the monks and clerks of the Middle Ages. These in turn handed it on to the humanists and school-masters of the Renaissance from whom it finally passed to the schools and universities of modern Europe and America.

This tradition is in many respects a unique one. It is distinguished from that of all the great oriental cultures by the fact that it was not confined to a priestly caste, or to the study of a sacred tradition, but formed an integral part of the life of the community. It grew up in the free atmosphere of the Greek city state, and its aim was to train men to be good citizens; to take their full share in the life and government of their city.

It was essentially a "liberal education" because it trained the free man in those "liberal arts" which were essential for the exercise of his proper function: above all, the art of speech and persuasion, an exact knowledge of the value of words and an understanding of the laws of thought and the rules of logic. Thus from the beginning the emphasis was on grammar and style and rhetoric, and there was a danger that education might be subordinated to utilitarian ends and regarded as a way of getting on in the world and achieving social success. But the Greeks were not unconscious of this danger, and from a comparatively early period the greatest minds of the Hellenic world devoted themselves to an inquiry into the true nature of education and into the ultimate philosophical issues that lie behind these problems.

This intense preoccupation with the theory of education reached its climax with Plato, whose dialogues are the most remarkable discussions of the subject in any age or literature. Plato had a revolutionary effect on Greek education, not so much by what he actually accomplished as an educator in the Academy as by the way in which he raised and widened the whole range of the discussion and introduced a new spiritual dimension to Greek culture.

Thenceforward the "liberal arts" of a purely civic education were not enough. They were but the preparation for the real business of higher education, which was to guide the mind by science and philosophy towards its final spiritual goal. And thus the Platonic Academy and the Aristotelian Lyceum created a new type of educational institution which was the archetype of the Western university. This tradition was maintained at Athens and later at Alexandria throughout the Hellenistic and Roman periods down to the closing of the schools by Justinian in 529 A.D.

But this form of higher education was not transmitted to the Latin West. Rome readily accepted the older tradition of civic education through the liberal arts, but she never fully assimilated the new philosophical ideals. A Roman like Cicero might study philosophy at Athens and Rhodes, but he remained fundamentally an orator, and in his treatise *de Oratore* he speaks of philosophy as one among the preparatory studies that are necessary to form the rhetorician. So too Quintilian stands for all that is best in the Roman tradition of education, but his doctrine is simply the traditional ideal of the liberal arts, and above all the art of rhetoric as a preparation for the full activities of a good citizen. But the tragedy of this educational ideal was that it had become divorced from social reality. The autonomous life of the free city state no longer existed, and what the new society needed was not orators and debaters but administrators and civil servants. The only point at which the traditional education met the needs of the existing social system was in the law courts, and its practical aim was to produce lawyers rather than statesmen.

In the Greek world, on the other hand, the loss of civic freedom had a stimulating effect, at least for a time, on the development of higher education. The philosophic ideals of a universal wisdom and an encyclopaedic science found their political corollary in the Hellenistic ideal of a universal state, and it was only fitting that Aristotle should have been the tutor of Alexander. Nevertheless the world expansion of Greek culture in the Hellenistic period failed to realize the higher aims that had been conceived by the great educationalists of the fourth century B.C. From the time of Plato the Hellenic *paideia* was a humanism in search for a theology, and the religious traditions of Greek culture were neither deep nor wide enough to provide the answer. The religious needs of the ancient world were satisfied not by philosophy but by the new religion which had emerged so suddenly and unpredictably from beneath the surface of the dominant culture. The coming of Christianity involved great cultural changes both socially and intellectually.

It created a new spiritual community which superseded, or at least limited, the old civic community, and it brought into the Roman world and the Hellenistic culture a new religious doctrine and a new religious literature.

It is true that this literature was not new in the absolute sense, for it was rooted in a tradition that was even more ancient than that of classical Hellenism, but in spite of the Septuagint and Philo it was still an unknown world to the Greeks and still more to the Romans. The new Christian culture was therefore built from the beginning on a double foundation. The old classical education in the liberal arts was maintained without any interruption, and since this education was inseparable from the study of the classical authors, the old classical literature continued to be studied. But alongside of—and above—all this, there was now a specifically Christian learning which was biblical and theological and which produced its own prolific literature.

We can study the process of transition in considerable detail. In the East the Cappadocian Fathers, St. Basil and the two Gregorys, studied at Athens with the leading pagan rhetoricians of their age, and their thought was influenced not only in its form by classical scholarship but in its content by Greek philosophy. In the West St. Augustine had been a professional rhetorician before his conversion and always retained his interest in educational problems, and though his knowledge of ancient philosophy was small in comparison with many of the Greek Fathers', he was a much more original thinker: one whose ideas have had a profound influence on the development of Western philosophy in every age down to our own.

Thus by the fifth century a synthesis had already been achieved between the two elements, and this remained the foundation of medieval culture and education. In the East, above all, this synthesis was the very soul of the Byzantine culture, which was at once essentially Greek and essentially Christian, which studied Homer and Plato as well as the Bible and the Fathers and maintained the tradition of an educated lay class throughout "the Dark Ages." Here, in contrast to the West, there was no break in the continuity of higher education, for the Palace School which was founded at Constantinople in 425 by Theodosius II was a regular state university which persisted, in spite of interruptions, for a thousand years and whose teachers included men of encyclopaedic learning, such as Photius in the ninth century and Michael Psellus in the eleventh.

In the West the situation was essentially different, since the fall of the Empire left the Church as the only surviving representative and guardian of Roman culture and Christian education. Here accordingly the liberal arts were preserved because they formed the necessary basis of the ecclesiastical studies without which the Church could not have survived. But in the new barbarian kingdoms the Church had to perform a far greater educational task than in the Byzantine world. Here she had to re-educate new peoples who were strangers to the life of the city and the higher civilization of the ancient world. The Greeks and the Romans had been prepared for Christianity by centuries of ethical teaching and discussion. Plato and Aristotle, Zeno and Epictetus and Marcus Aurelius had familiarized men with the ideas of man's spiritual nature, the immortality of the soul, divine providence and human responsibility. But the barbarians knew none of this. Their moral ideals were still derived from the primitive heroic ethics of tribal society: virtue was military valor and loyalty, justice was revenge, religion was an instinctive veneration of the dark forces that manifest themselves in the life of the earth and the fates of men and peoples.

Thus the main effort of the Church had to be directed towards moral education, to the establishment of a new order resting on a faith in divine providence and on the spiritual and moral responsibility of the human soul towards God.

In comparison with this central task, the transmission of the intellectual heritage of the ancient world, as embodied in the traditional forms of liberal education, was of secondary importance. Nevertheless it was essential to preserve this educational tradition, in order to prevent the Church from becoming absorbed by its barbarian environment. Latin was the language of the liturgy and the Bible, and in the new lands it had to be acquired by men who had no immediate contact with the Latin-speaking world. Thus the Church had a direct utilitarian interest in the maintenance of the educational tradition, and the Latin grammar followed the Gospels into the forests of the North and the remote islands of the Western ocean. This new Latin ecclesiastical culture found its center in the monasteries which almost from the beginning were schools of Christian learning, as well as schools of the Christian way of life. The last achievement of classical culture in Italy was the plan of monastic studies which Cassiodorus, the Roman aristocrat and ex-consul, laid down in his monastery at Vivarium in the second half of the sixth century, and the same tradition is represented half a century later by St. Isidore of Seville, whose encyclopaedic works had an enormous influence on medieval education.

This idea of using the old liberal classical education in the service of the Church and ecclesiastical learning was diffused throughout Western Europe by the monastic movement. It had already reached Ireland by the sixth century, and in the following century it inspired the new Christian culture of Anglo-Saxon England, whence it was re-transmitted to continental

Europe by St. Boniface and Alcuin and became the main source of the Carolingian revival of learning. But already by the beginning of the eighth century this tradition of Christian education had achieved very remarkable results. The Venerable Bede was a scholar of whom any age might be proud, and the rapid flowering of this new Latin Christian culture on barbarian soil shows that the combination of the old tradition of liberal education with the dynamic moral energy of Christianity was not an archaic survival of a dead culture but a vital process which was capable of giving birth to the new forms of culture. And this process extended far beyond the limits of formal education into the underlying stratum of native barbarian society where it gave birth to a new art and a new vernacular Christian literature.

II. THE AGE OF THE UNIVERSITIES
AND THE RISE OF VERNACULAR
CULTURE

Throughout the early Middle Ages Western education followed the lines that had been laid down in the last period of the Roman Empire. It was based on Latin grammar, on the study of the Latin classics, the Latin Fathers and the Bible and the Liturgy. It was therefore a specifically clerical education which was normally confined to the monastic and cathedral schools, although it might also be found in the palace schools of the more enlightened rulers like Charlemagne, who did a great service to the cause of Christian culture by his educational capitularies, in which he insists on the importance of a high standard of accuracy in the copying of manuscripts and the use of correct texts.

But it was left to King Alfred of Wessex in the dark days that followed the breakdown of the Carolingian Empire to put forward the new ideal of a vernacular Christian education for all free men, laymen as well as clerics. He had seen the old centers of monastic culture destroyed by the new barbarian invasions, and he used the brief breathing-space between his endless wars to make a little library of Christian classics in English, "changing into the language we all know the books that are most needful to be known by all men; and we will bring it about, as we very well may if we have peace, that all the youth of free men in England, those that have the opportunity to give themselves to it, should be bound to learning, while they can be bound to no other usefulness, until the time when they all know how to read English writing."[1] His selection consists of St. Gregory's *Pastoral Care* and his *Dialogues* (which contains the life of St. Benedict), the *Universal History* of Orosius, Bede's *Ecclesiastical History of the English People*, Boethius' *Consolation of Philosophy* and an anthology containing the first part of St. Augustine's *Soliloquies* together with other passages from the Fathers and some of his own composition. Taken as a whole, it is a remarkable choice for a warrior king and suggests quite an original conception of a liberal education based on history and natural theology, rather than on grammar and rhetoric.

But this was the isolated effort of an original mind which had little influence on future developments. The continuity of culture was maintained chiefly by the great monasteries of Germany, Fulda, Corvey, Reichenau and St. Gall, and by the Cathedral schools of Gaul which took an increasingly important part in education from the beginning of the eleventh century. This development culminated in the twelfth century in a great revival of studies which had a revolutionary effect on the history of Western education. It has often been described as "the Renaissance of the Twelfth Century," and it resembles the later Italian Renaissance in its passionate devotion to the cause of learning and its boundless veneration for the thought of the ancient classical world.

But this medieval renaissance differs from its successor in that its interests centered in Greek philosophy and science rather

[1] Preface to Gregory's *Pastoral Care*, tr. by M. Williams.

than in literature. During its earlier phase as represented by the school of Chartres, the tradition of the liberal arts was still predominant, as we see in the writings of John of Salisbury, who was a humanist *avant le nom*, but John himself was one of the first to point out the importance of the "New Logic" of Aristotle, above all the Topics, which transformed the old scholastic logic into a new kind of scientific thought. The recovery of the works of Aristotle, which reached Western Europe first through the medium of Arabic thought and the translators of the school of Toledo, marks an epoch in Western thought. And Aristotle did not come alone; he was the greatest amongst a whole galaxy of Greek and Arabic philosophers and scientists and mathematicians—Ptolemy, Euclid, Avicenna, Al Farabi, Albategni and others—whose works were translated at the same time. The men of the West suddenly realized the existence of a world of thought which had been unknown to them and the power of human reason to explore these new fields of knowledge.

But how was this new knowledge to be reconciled with the religious tradition of Western Christendom and the educational traditions of monastic schools? The dangers of a conflict were shown in the first half of the twelfth century by St. Bernard's attack on the new dialectical theology of Abelard, and it was increased in the following decades by the wholesale importation of Graeco-Arabic works which had no roots in the Christian past and seemed irreconcilable with Catholic dogma. But the intellectual and spiritual forces of Christian culture were strong enough to meet the challenge.

It was an age of intense creative activity which saw the rise of the communes, the foundation of the new religious orders, the building of the great Gothic cathedrals and the creation of a new poetry. And so too, under the impact of new knowledge, Western education not only transformed its curriculum of studies, it also created new intellectual organs and new social institutions which have had a lasting influence on the development of Western education. As the late Dr. Rashdall wrote: "Through all the changes which have taken place in the subject matter and the methods of the education regarded at the highest from the twelfth century down to the present time, that education has continued to be given through the machinery supplied by a distinctively medieval institution—an institution which still, even in the minute details of its organization, continues to exhibit its continuity with its two great thirteenth century prototypes, medieval Paris and medieval Bologna."[1]

The nature of the medieval university may perhaps be best understood in relation to the contemporary development of the commune and the guild. Though it developed from the traditional institution of the cathedral school, it was essentially a free, self-governing guild of scholars which possessed a charter of privilege and its own organs of government. Indeed the word *universitas* was commonly used like *communitas* to describe any free corporate body, and what we call a university was usually described as *studium generale*, a place of study that was not merely local but open to students from other cities and countries. The University of Paris, which was the oldest *studium generale* of Northern Europe and the greatest center of theological and philosophical studies in Christendom, was a corporation of "masters" or graduates who had received the license to teach, and it consisted of the four faculties of Theology, Canon Law, Medicine and Arts, the last of which was divided into four separately organized Nations.

[1] *Cambridge Medieval History*, vol. vi, p. 601.

The University of Bologna, which was even older than Paris and the chief center of legal studies in the West was, on the other hand, a corporation of students, in which the professors, who had a separate collegiate organization, had no direct responsibility or control.

All the later medieval universities followed one or other of these models, the earliest of them, Oxford, being a corporation of masters on the Parisian model and equally devoted to theological and philosophical studies.

The result of these new institutions was to give higher education a degree of prestige and social influence that it had not possessed since the Hellenistic age. The great schools like Paris and Bologna possessed an international position. They recruited students from all over Western Europe and gave them a common sense of intellectual values and of their own corporate strength. They formed an intellectual élite—or *intelligentsia*—which was almost independent of wealth and birth, since many of them were poor and of humble origin. It is true that university education was expensive in time if in no other respect, and few of the students who matriculated in the faculty of Arts in their early teens could afford the full six years of study for the M.A. degree, still less for the further twelve years that were necessary in order to obtain the doctorate. But those who could stay the course and reach the dignity of Doctor of Divinity at Paris or Oxford, or Doctor of Civil Law at Bologna, were in a position to attain the highest offices in Church and State.

Thus whatever we may think of the value of the content of medieval education, there can be no doubt of its cultural importance as an intellectual discipline that moulded the Western mind, and this was clearly recognized in the Middle Ages when

Studium, or Learning, was ranked alongside of *Imperium* and *Sacerdotium*—Empire and Priesthood—as one of the three great powers that ruled the Christian world. Thus in the four-teenth and fifteenth centuries when the unity of Christendom was broken by the Great Schism, we see the University of Paris intervening decisively in the solution of the conflict, and its leading doctors like the Chancellors Gerson and Peter d'Ailly become for a time the most important figures in Christendom.

But what of the new knowledge and thought which were the intellectual substance of the medieval university? In modern times they have often been treated with contempt. "Scholasti-cism" became a term of abuse, and the Christian-Aristotelian synthesis was regarded as the embodiment of obscurantism and traditionalism. Men did not realize what a tremendous signifi-cance Aristotle had for medieval civilization. He stood not only for the idea of science and scientific method, but also for a new science of nature and man which was the gateway to a whole world of knowledge and finally for the metaphysical ideal of a super-science which provided a rational basis for theology. And, as I have said, Aristotle did not come alone: his influence was reinforced by a whole scientific and philosophic literature which brought back to the West the higher learning of the Greek and Oriental worlds. Thus to thirteenth-century Europe, Aristotle stood not for traditionalism but for the spirit of in-novation, and the real danger was that the new wine would burst the old bottles and that Western culture would be divided by a conflict between rational philosophy and traditional theol-ogy, as actually occurred in the Islamic world at this time. This danger was averted by the new medieval university, and above all by the Christian Aristotelianism of St. Thomas, which has remained the classical expression of Catholic philosophy.

But this achievement was not simply due to the university. On the contrary it met considerable resistance from the conservative element both at Paris and Oxford. It was the result of the union of the new learning with the religious spirit of the new international teaching orders; above all the Dominicans and the Franciscans—which found in the medieval university an ideal field for the development of their intellectual apostolate. It was through these new orders that the old monastic ideal of the consecration of learning to the Christian way of life was renewed and raised to a higher intellectual plane. Hence the great age of medieval scholasticism was also the great age of medieval mysticism, and the aridity of the method of logical disputation was transcended by the higher contemplative knowledge of spiritual reality. The medieval mind was always conscious of man's final end and the goal of his intellectual and moral pilgrimage, as Dante sees it in the great concluding passage of his poem.

Nevertheless, though the example of Dante shows that the new philosophical culture was capable of the highest literary and aesthetic achievement, it must be admitted that the advance in philosophy and science was accompanied by a decline in the general literary standards of Western education. The substitution of the study of Aristotle for the study of the Latin classics which took place in the Arts course in the medieval university included a serious set-back for the cause of humanism which Professor Gilson has termed *"l'exil des belles-lettres."* This tendency was foreseen and combated by the greatest English scholar of the twelfth century, John of Salisbury, in his long polemic against the Philistines. In his view everything depends on the "sweet and fruitful marriage of Reason and the Word" which is the source of human civilization, and without which men become brutalized and the city degenerates into a herd of human animals. It is true that his enemies are not so much the Aristotelians as the clerical utilitarians who were intent on using education as a means of getting on in the world; and there is no doubt that this type was common enough in the medieval universities. The sudden growth of the new schools in the twelfth and thirteenth centuries was a sort of intellectual gold rush and produced an extraordinarily vital, disorderly, tumultuous democracy which resembled the society of a mining camp rather than the disciplined academic life of the modern university.

But though the humanist tradition was divorced from the new scientific-metaphysical culture of the medieval university, it was not lost. It found a new field of expansion in the vernacular literatures which were being created at the same period that saw the rise of the universities. Dante's apologia had been preceded by two centuries of experiment and experience in French and Provençal poetry, and already in the twelfth century poets like Arnaut Daniel in the South and Chrétien de Troyes in the North prove the existence of a highly advanced literary tradition. This tradition was quite distinct from that of the universities and the monastic schools. It had its center in the life of the feudal courts which were so numerous in the Middle Ages, and which gave their name to the new moral and social ideal that inspired the new vernacular literature. *Curialitas,* or "courtesy," was to the Middle Ages what *civilitas,* or "politeness," was to the ancient city state. It was the quality that characterized the good knight or the "gentle man" as *civilitas* characterized the citizen and the free man.

This "courtly" culture was by no means a simple thing. As I

have shown elsewhere,[1] it represents the coalescence of a number of different elements which came together in Western Europe in the age of the Crusades. On the one hand there were the old traditions of the heroic age of the North which still lived on in the Anglo-Saxon epic and the northern sagas—the common life of the chief and his followers who feasted together in the great hall and listened to the minstrels singing of the deeds of the heroes and the story of the past. And on the other hand there was the new poetry and music which came up from the South at the time of the Crusades, the art of the troubadours who sang of love and the service of ladies and who created that elaborate code of manners and morals which became the standard of "chivalry" and "courtesy." And finally there was the influence of Latin and classical culture which brought Ovid into the world of the troubadours and Alexander and Aeneas into the world of Charlemagne and Arthur.

Thus at the same time that the higher clerical education was being transformed by Aristotle and the universities, lay education was undergoing a parallel process of change which transformed the barbarian feudal warrior into the medieval knight. It has often been questioned whether this cult of chivalry had any profound influence on the behavior and morality of the ruling classes in medieval society. But there can be no doubt of its importance as a literary influence. It affected every form of vernacular literature from the eleventh to the sixteenth century, even on the most popular levels. It influenced not only Dante and Petrarch and Chaucer, but the lays of the minstrels and the ballads of the people. Above all it had a profound influence on religion, so that from St. Francis onwards the poetry and spiritual experiences of mystics like Ramon Lull, Jacopone da Todi,

[1] *Medieval Essays* (New York, Sheed & Ward, 1954).

Mechtild of Magdeburg, Henry Suso and many more were colored by the imagery and ideology of the courtly culture.

It is difficult to overestimate the importance of this element in medieval culture. It spread through a hundred different channels into every part of Europe and affected all classes of the population. Above all it exercised a civilizing and educative influence on the ruling classes, who regarded learning as the business of the clerks and whose energies were devoted to war and to the chase. It brought the code of honor from the battlefield into the details of social life and taught the knight to appreciate poetry and music and the art of the spoken and written word. The best thirteenth-century writers, at least in northern Europe, were not the scholars who had enjoyed the advantages of a university education, but laymen and soldiers, nobles or courtiers, like Conon of Bethune and Thibaut of Champagne, Villehardouin and Joinville, Wolfram von Eschenbach and Snorri Sturlason and Walter von der Vogelweide.

Hence this vernacular tradition formed an essential part of the Christian culture of the West. It is true that it was not Christian in the same sense as the old ecclesiastical and monastic tradition, since it embodied considerable non-Christian elements, but in a sense it was more significant, since it shows how the native tradition of the semi-barbaric West had become modified and transformed in the course of centuries by the influence of Christian culture.

The subsequent development of European culture and Western education was conditioned by the coming together of these two traditions, and it was this synthesis, no less than the recovery of Greek literature, which explains the origins of the Italian Renaissance. The rise of the city states in medieval Italy had created a society in which nobles and clerks and bourgeois met on almost equal terms, since the noble was a citizen and the bourgeois was a clerk. Thus nobles like Guido Cavalcanti cultivated the poetry and ideals of the courtly culture, while the civic officials were often university men who had been trained in the schools of Bologna and Padua.

In the fourteenth century these two traditions of culture were united not only in the same culture but in the same individuals. Dante used the "sweet new style" of the vernacular courtly poetry to give literary expression to the vast cosmic and theological synthesis which had been created by St. Thomas and his predecessors in the medieval university. Petrarch, on the other hand, in spite of his high achievement as a vernacular courtly poet, made it his life work to revive the tradition of classical Latin studies which had been temporarily interrupted by the triumph of Aristotelian scholasticism. From his boyhood he had been a lover of Cicero, in whose writings he found that perfect union of thought and language of which John of Salisbury spoke, and he regarded the victory of the scholastic dialecticians as a new barbarian invasion that was equally dangerous to Latin culture and Christian traditions. Against them he invoked the tradition of the Fathers, above all St. Augustine, whom he regarded as the supreme representative of Christian philosophy.

We should note that there is no justification here for the popular notion that the Renaissance was an irreligious neo-pagan movement. Certainly there was a strong current of rationalist and unorthodox ideas in fourteenth-century Italy, but if we are to believe Petrarch, the chief representatives of this tendency were to be found not among the humanists but among the philosophers and the scientists, above all the Averroists of Padua, against whom so much of Petrarch's polemics are directed. The return to antiquity, as advocated by Petrarch himself and by his disciple Coluccio Salutati, the Chancellor of the Florentine Republic, and by Leonardo Bruni of Arezzo, was also a return to Christian antiquity and to the traditional alliance of classical and patristic studies.

Thus by the fourteenth century the division in Western culture was no longer one between a vernacular courtly tradition and a Latin ecclesiastical one, nor yet one between a neo-pagan renaissance and the medieval Christian traditionalism, but rather between the humanists and the scientists, both of whom claimed to stand for the cause of true learning and Christian truth. The dominant trend of thought in the universities which were now spreading all over Europe from Spain and Scotland to Germany and Bohemia was not the Augustinianism of St. Bonaventura or the Christian Aristotelianism of St. Thomas, but the *via modernorum* of William of Ockham and his disciples.

This new school did not create any great metaphysical synthesis. It was concerned above all with questions of method and with the criticism of traditional ideas. It emphasized the importance of direct intuitive knowledge—the knowledge of the singular—the use of the inductive method, and the principle of economy, all of which were to become the principles of the new science of nature. Thus the fourteenth-century philosophers by their criticism of Aristotelian physics and their conception of the experimental method laid the foundations for the Copernican revolution of the future, as we see above all in the writings of Nicholas of Oresme, a remarkable and many-sided thinker,[1] who was the first man to propound a clear statement of the

[1] In addition to his writings on physics, he translated Aristotle's *Politics* and *Ethics* into French and wrote a treatise on coinage, *De l'origine, nature et mutation des monnaies,* which is perhaps the earliest work on monetary questions.

objections to the accepted Ptolemaic geocentric theory of the movement of the heavens. Thus the conflict between the humanists and the schoolmen was by no means a simple opposition of intellectual progress to unintelligent traditionalism as was believed in the centuries that followed. For in many respects the later scholasticism was more original and more critical in method and spirit than the humanism which was inspired by a blind veneration of classical antiquity.

Nevertheless the original development of philosophical and scientific studies which had its center in the northern universities, above all at Paris and Oxford, did not survive the fourteenth century. It was essentially an international movement, the intellectual expression of that great movement towards spiritual unity which had inspired all the characteristic achievements of medieval culture and had reached its climax in the thirteenth century.

But at the end of the fourteenth century this unity was in process of dissolution. The alliance between the Papacy and the monastic reformers which had created the thirteenth-century unity had broken down. The Church was divided by schism, and the focal areas of medieval culture were being devastated by the endless conflict of the Hundred Years' War and the internecine feud between France and Burgundy. The Conciliar movement of the early fifteenth century represents the final effort of medieval Christendom to recover its lost unity, when the universities, above all the University of Paris, attempted to assert the supremacy of *Studium* as the supreme arbiter of the Christian world. The failure of this movement marks the end of the Middle Ages, and with its failure the leadership of Western culture passed from the North to Italy, and from the schoolmen to the humanists.

III. THE AGE OF HUMANISM

The higher culture of modern Europe, and of America also, has been formed by the educational tradition that had its roots in the Italian Renaissance. It was a tradition that had its center not so much in the universities, which long retained their medieval character, but rather in the academies and the learned societies, in the Jesuit colleges and the English public schools. Today this tradition has lost its intellectual supremacy and its social prestige, but it still lives in the cultures it created, for all the modern vernacular literatures, from Shakespeare and Milton to Goethe and Hölderlin, are its children.

But at the present time the importance of the Italian Renaissance and the value of the humanist culture are less regarded than they have been for more than four hundred years. It would be difficult to find anyone today who would agree with Voltaire's judgment that the age of Pope Leo X was one of those rare moments in the life of humanity which "vindicate the greatness of the human spirit and compensate the historian for the barren prospect of a thousand years of stupidity and barbarism." Nevertheless the Italian Renaissance marks a turning point in history, due to a change in the axis of Western culture, which no historian can afford to ignore. The focus of medieval Christendom was to be found in the North, in the territories between the Rhine and the Loire, which was the source of almost all the characteristic achievements of the Middle Ages. This was the center of the Carolingian Empire and the French monarchy and the feudal society. It was the source of the great movements of monastic and ecclesiastical reform, and of the Crusading movement. It was the cradle of Gothic architecture and of the medieval schools of scholastic philosophy.

But in the later Middle Ages a new kind of society was growing up in Italy and the Mediterranean which was radically different from the feudal-ecclesiastical society of the North. It was a society of cities and city states in which the political conception of citizenship took the place of the feudal relation of personal allegiance and loyalty, so that it tended to reproduce the old patterns of classical Mediterranean city culture. As the unity of medieval Christendom became weaker and the old northern center of medieval culture declined, the revival of Mediterranean culture grew in strength and became increasingly conscious of its independent origins and of the great traditions of the past. This consciousness was increased by the fact that the Italian cities had become the dominant power in the Eastern Mediterranean and were thus brought into immediate contact with the older traditions of the Byzantine Empire and of Greek culture. Venice and Genoa were the rulers of the Aegean and the Ionian Seas, a Florentine dynasty reigned at Athens and the Byzantine emperors themselves were being forced by the Turkish peril to lay aside their hostility to the Latins and look to Venice and the Papacy for help.

Thus at the very moment when, as I mentioned in the last chapter, the final breach occurred between the Papacy and the Conciliar movement, which had been led by the University of Paris, a rapprochement was taking place between Rome and Constantinople which led to the reunion of the Eastern and Western Churches at the Council of Florence in 1439. It is true that the Union failed to gain popular support in the East and consequently failed to save the Byzantine Empire. But nevertheless it produced a rapprochement between the leading minds of the new Italian culture and the last representatives of Byzantine Hellenism.

For Greek culture in the last days of the Byzantine Empire was not so decadent as one might have expected from its political decline. There were even signs of a cultural revival which was inspired by Hellenic rather than Byzantine traditions. But conditions in the East were unfavorable to its development, and the outlying provinces of the Byzantine world, such as Russia, were far too backward to carry on the traditions of Greek culture.

Consequently it was in Italy and not in the East that the soil was ripe to receive the seeds of Hellenism. The Italian cities resembled the city states of ancient Greece in the intensity of their political life, the activity of their artistic impulse and the keenness of their intellectual interests. Above all the life of the Italian city reproduced the same conditions under which the Greek *paideia* had originally developed—the need for an education that would train the citizen in the "liberal arts" that would fit him for public life and the existence of a critical audience that could appreciate the art of the orator, the poet and the historian. It was to this world that the last representatives of the higher culture of the Byzantine world brought back the riches of Greek literature and scholarship which had been lost to the West for a thousand years.

Ever since the Council of Lyons in the thirteenth century Byzantine men of learning had visited the West as ambassadors. At the end of the thirteenth century the editor of the Greek Anthology, Maximus Planudes, had been the Byzantine ambassador at Venice, and in the following century Demetrius Cydones had not only worked for the union of the churches but had introduced the work of St. Thomas to the Byzantine world. But it was with the coming of Manuel Chrysoloras at the end of the fourteenth century that the influence of Greek culture on Italian education first became fully effective. As ambassador at Venice, lecturer at Florence and Padua and teacher of the leading Italian scholars of his age, he was the man who first broke down the barrier that had cut off Western Christendom from a direct knowledge of Greek culture. Henceforward intellectual relations between East and West were increasingly frequent and intimate and reached their climax when the Council of 1439 brought the Emperor and the Patriarch and all the leading representatives of Byzantine culture to Florence. Some of them made their home in Italy, above all Cardinal Bessarion, who became one of the leading figures in Renaissance Italy. Bessarion was the chief representative of Byzantine Platonism, and no one did more to encourage that revival of Platonic studies in Italy, which was hardly less important for the history of Western culture than the rediscovery of Aristotle two or three centuries earlier. And as the coming of Aristotle involved a recovery of the Greek scientific tradition, so the coming of Plato was accompanied by the rediscovery of Greek poetry and drama and history. In a certain sense this second renaissance was less revolutionary than the earlier one, since though it enlarged the scope of liberal education it did not change its nature. It was a return to the tradition of John of Salisbury and the school of Chartres which had already accepted the ideal of *humanitas* and which looked to Plato rather than to Aristotle as the source of their philosophy. The Platonism of Marsilio Ficino and his Academy at Florence which exercised such an enormous influence on the thought of the Italian Renaissance was very close to the spirit of Bernard Silvestris and the school of Chartres, though the latter knew Plato only through the *Timaeus* and the *Phaedo*, whereas the former knew him in the original, together with Plotinus and the works of the Neoplatonic commentators.

But from the educational point of view the change was enormous. Hellenism brought back into higher education the aesthetic and moral elements which had been lost in the scientific disputations of the schoolmen, although it survived on the vernacular level in the courtly culture. Now the humanists learnt from Xenophon and Plato and Isocrates that education was an art which should aim at the harmonious development of every side of human nature, physical, moral and intellectual. Thus they gained an awareness of the unlimited possibilities of the enrichment of personal life by art and literature and social intercourse.

It was in the light of these ideas that the tradition of humanist education developed, and for more than a century from the beginning of the fifteenth century to the middle of the sixteenth, there was more thinking and writing on educational subjects than at any time since the great age of Hellenic culture. But though this movement was inspired by an intense devotion to classical culture it was not conscious of any disloyalty to the Christian tradition. The great humanist educators, like Leonardo Bruni, Guarino of Verona, Vittorino da Feltre, P. P. Vergerio and Maffeo Vegio were themselves devout Christians who wished to unite the intellectual and aesthetic culture of Hellenism with the spiritual ideals of Christianity. This Christian aspect of the Renaissance culture has been seriously underestimated by the nineteenth-century historians of Renaissance culture, and especially by the greatest of them, Jacob Burckhardt, and this has evoked a somewhat exaggerated reaction on the part of modern writers like Conrad Burdach and G. Toffanin.

Perhaps the most moderate and just statement is that of an English educationalist scholar, the late W. H. Woodward, who made a special study of the educational aspects of humanism. "It cannot be too strongly affirmed," he writes, "that a close acquaintance with the actual work of Vittorino and Guarino, and with the aims of Vergerius and Vegio, reveals a thorough sincerity of religious conviction which permeates all their educational practice. Vittorino's great achievement was to effect a reconciliation between the Christian life and Humanist ideals; in this he was followed by other masters, though rarely with the same unfaltering consistency. It is a fair description of the motive underlying Vittorino's method that he regarded Humanist education as the training for Christian citizenship. He himself took a leading part in the religious teaching of the school; and by addresses, by private conversations, and above all by his own example, he brought the full force of his personal character to bear upon his pupils in the critical years of their life. He expressly encouraged a sense of responsibility towards the poor and suffering and never forgot his civic obligation, and its religious sanction."[1]

But the most remarkable attempt to assert the essential agreement of Christianity and Hellenism is to be found in the life and work of Marsilio Ficino and the group of scholars and men of culture who formed the Platonic Academy at Florence in the second half of the fifteenth century. It was their aim to do for Plato and Plotinus what the thirteenth century had done for Aristotle, and though they were far inferior to the great me-

[1] *Vittorino da Feltre and Other Humanist Educators* (Cambridge, 1897), p. 242.

dieval thinkers as metaphysicians and theologians, they were
highly successful in the field of culture, and the Christian
Platonism which they revived rather than created became for
two centuries the accepted philosophy of humanism.

At the same time they created a new institution which became
the chief organ of the new humanist culture. The whole of the
Renaissance and Baroque periods was the age of the academies,
and the academy was essentially a private association of scholars
and amateurs who met to discuss scientific as well as literary
questions. Throughout the next two centuries it was these
associations which were the centers of the higher culture, while
the universities remained the strongholds of medieval educational traditions and of intellectual vested interests. This was
not so at the beginning, at least in Italy. In the fourteenth century the University of Florence showed a remarkable awareness
of contemporary culture when it established a chair for Boc-
caccio to lecture on Dante, which is rather as though Cambridge
had endowed a chair of Shakespearian studies with Milton as its
first professor! And throughout the fifteenth and sixteenth centuries the Italian universities, especially those of Florence,
Padua and Ferrara, played an important part in the development of the new learning and in the beginnings of modern scientific studies.

North of the Alps also the influence of the Italian Renaissance was first felt in university circles, and the leaders of the
movement in Germany, France and England, Reuchlin, Erasmus, Lefèvre d'Etaples, Fisher and John Colet, still represented
the medieval tradition of clerical learning and ecclesiastical
society. Consequently it is not surprising that the Christian
aspect of the Renaissance was even more strongly accentuated
here than in the South, and the influence of Christian Platonism

and of the Florentine Academy was stronger than that of the purely literary humanism of Poggio and Valla. But although this Northern humanism was overtly and consciously Christian, it aroused much sharper opposition from the representatives of the old order than was the case in Italy. The literary quarrels that were so numerous and bitter between the Italian scholars became transformed in the Gothic North into an ideological warfare between the conservatives and the modernists in which the latter used the weapons of ridicule and vituperation against the monks and the theologians, while the conservatives responded with accusations of heresy and ecclesiastical censures.

For these reasons the Northern humanists have been regarded as the forerunners and even the originators of the Reformation. And to a certain extent this is true. It was the humanists who began the public campaign against the corruptions and superstitions of the late medieval Church, and it was the greatest of them all, Erasmus of Rotterdam, who began the propaganda for a return to Christian antiquity and to the pure evangelical Christianity of the New Testament. Nevertheless the spirit of the German Reformation was entirely different from that of Erasmus, and when its character became plain, no one was more horrified than the humanists. It was a revolutionary movement of the most far-reaching kind which embodied all the elements in Northern Europe that were most alien from the ideals of the new humanist culture of the Mediterranean world. Its great leader, Martin Luther, was the supreme example of the anti-humanist spirit, the enemy of moderation and human reason, an individualist who denied human freedom, a man of passion who condemned nature, a conservative who rejected tradition.

This inherent contradiction between Protestantism and Humanism became overt in the early years of the Reformation in the controversy between Luther and Erasmus on the Freedom of the Will, which led to a bitter antagonism between the two leaders and to the progressive estrangement of the German Reformation from the humanist culture. In this field, however, the success of Luther was far less complete than in the sphere of religion and politics. He destroyed the spiritual unity of medieval Christendom, the Roman order and the Catholic hierarchy together with the institutions and beliefs on which medieval culture had been founded, above all the monastic orders, which had been for centuries the chief representatives of the higher culture and the teachers of the Christian people. And by so doing, there was generated, for the first time in Western history, a revolutionary attitude towards the past and to the inherited norms of culture. As Döllinger wrote, the new generation in the schools and universities "were taught to despise past generations and consequently their own ancestors as men wilfully plunged in error" and to believe "that the Popes and bishops, the theologians and the universities, the monasteries and all the teaching corporations had formed for centuries a vast conspiracy to deform and suppress the teaching of the Gospel."[1]

This revolutionary change was even more serious than we can realize today, owing to its destructive effects on the mind of the masses and the education of the common people. In the Middle Ages that education had never been a matter of book learning. The main channels of Christian culture were liturgical and artistic. The life of the community centered in the Church, in the performance of the liturgy and the cult of the Saints. The annual cycle of feasts and fasts was the background of social

[1] Döllinger, *The Reformation in Its Relations with the Schools and Universities and the Education of Youth in the Reformation*, vol. i, p. 397. (French trans.)

life, and every vital moment in the life of the community found in it an appropriate ritual and sacramental expression. Architecture and painting and sculpture, music and poetry were all enlisted in its service, and no one was too poor or too uneducated to share in its mysteries.

Now all this was swept away in the course of a single generation and a new Protestant culture had to be built up based almost exclusively on the study of the Bible and the dogmatic theology of the new sects. There was a complete ideological separation between Catholic and Protestant Europe. Truth in one country was heresy in another; even the fundamental conceptions of the Christian life, of moral perfection, of sanctity and salvation were different.

If therefore the religious revolution of the Reformation had developed to its logical conclusion, there can be no doubt that Western Europe would have ceased to exist as a cultural unity. There would have been two completely separate cultures in the Protestant North and the Catholic South, divided by an iron curtain of persecution and repression which would have made the two parts of Europe as alien and incomprehensible from one another as Christendom was from Islam.

It was the influence of the humanist education that saved Europe from this fate. The extremism of Luther himself and the fanaticism of the left wing of the Reformation were not strong enough to overcome the influence of humanism and clerical culture which broke the iron curtain of religious conflict and created an educational ideal that was common to both worlds.

For there were humanists in both camps from the first, and in spite of their theological opposition they remained in substantial agreement in their educational ideals and their concept of humane learning. It is true that the majority of the Northern humanists followed the example of Erasmus and soon lost whatever sympathies they had with the Protestant Reformers. But there were exceptions to this rule, especially in the younger generation, and the most important of these exceptions, Melanchthon, did all in his power to check the breakdown of culture and to establish a sound tradition of Protestant education. But his success was a very limited one, for German humanism never recovered from the shock of the Reformation. In the West, however, the situation was different. French Protestantism from the first found wide support in humanist circles. Calvin himself fully appreciated the importance of education and study. Wherever the Calvinists went, from Transylvania to Massachusetts, they brought with them not only the Bible and Calvin's *Institutes*, but the Latin grammar and the study of the classics.

Meanwhile in Catholic Europe the influence of Christian humanism continued to develop. The leaders of Catholic culture in the age of the Reformation, like Cardinal Sadoleto and Cardinal Pole, maintained the traditions of the fifteenth century, and Sadoleto's treatise *de liberis recte instituendis* (1530) explains the educational ideals of humanism in their most mature form. After the Council of Trent the situation was changed by the Counter-Reformation and the drastic measures that were taken to repress Protestantism and to reassert the control of the Church over literature and education. But there was no breach in the continuity of culture such as occurred in the North. The tradition of popular culture remained unchanged, and the Church used the new art and music and drama as the Church of the Middle Ages had done in the past. It was this permeation of Renaissance art and literature by the religious spirit of the Catholic revival which gave birth to the Baroque culture which in the seventeenth century spread over the whole of Catholic Europe and extended its influence into the North, in very much the same way as the Gothic art and culture had expanded four centuries earlier, in the opposite direction.

The carriers of this culture were the new religious orders, above all the Society of Jesus, which played a similar part in European culture in the later sixteenth and seventeenth centuries to that which the Benedictines had played in the early Middle Ages or the Franciscans and Dominicans in the thirteenth century. Like them, the Jesuits owed their influence above all to their educational activities; and as the Benedictines had based their teaching on an adaptation of the classical education of the later Roman Empire to Christian aims, so now the Jesuits adapted the new classical education of the humanists of the Renaissance to the religious ideals of the Counter-Reformation. The Jesuit *Ratio Studiorum* belongs to the same tradition as that of the humanist treatises on education of which I have spoken above. It was, however, more limited and more practical in its aims. Its originality lay in its technique and organization rather than in its subject matter. Nevertheless it did more than anything else to establish a common international standard of higher education, so that even in Protestant Europe the Jesuit schools met with the approval of such a revolutionary critic of education as Francis Bacon.[1]

Thus under the influence of humanism, Catholic and Protestant Europe shared a common type of culture. The educated classes studied the same languages in the same way, read the same books and accepted the same ideal pattern of "the scholar and

[1] "As for the Pedagogical part, the shortest rule would be 'consult the schools of the Jesuits,' for nothing better has been put in practice." Bacon, *de Augmentis Scientiarum*, Bk. VI, ch. iv.

the gentleman" which had been laid down in the standard courtesy books of the Italian Renaissance—above all in Baldassare Castiglione's book of *The Courtier* (1528), which was translated into almost every Western European language. In spite of the religious divisions of Europe, the world of learning and literature and art remained an international community, so that even during the Wars of Religion, scholars and scientists corresponded with one another, and Englishmen and Germans continued to visit Italy, like Milton, and to study at Padua, like William Harvey.

This persistence of the unity of Western culture in spite of the disunity of Christendom is to be seen in a field where one might have expected the forces of disunity to be the strongest. I mean in the vernacular literatures. The new national literatures naturally reflect the growing divergence of the new national states; yet at the same time they all embody the same humanist culture, derived from the same sources and governed by the same principles of criticism and style. The mutual intercourse of the vernacular literatures of the sixteenth and seventeenth centuries by translation, imitation and unacknowledged borrowing is so universal that it is impossible to understand any one of these literatures apart from the rest. They form one great literature, diffused throughout the West in the different vernacular languages from Italy to France and Spain and Portugal, and from Italy and France to England and Germany and Holland.

Through these vernacular literatures, the humanist tradition reached down to the level of popular culture until it eventually reached every man who could read. And owing to the introduction of printing and the multiplication of books, the literate classes long had ceased to be identified with the clerical profession. They included the whole of the upper and middle classes and a considerable number of artisans and even peasants. In this respect Protestantism, with its insistence on the reading of the Bible in the vernacular, had a very considerable influence on the growth of literacy among the Puritans and the independent sects which based their appeal on the conscience of the individual believer. Consequently the Puritans everywhere paid considerable attention to educational matters, so that in New England, for example, the educational legislation of 1642 and 1647 is in advance of its age, although the education that it envisaged was purely religious and utilitarian and did not share the humanist spirit that dominated vernacular literature in Europe. "What schoolboy, what apprentice," asks an English writer of 1620, "knows not Heliodorus?" But it is safe to say that the New England schoolboy knew neither Heliodorus nor Shakespeare, nor even Milton. He learnt his letters in order to read the Bible and the Puritan divines.

But the narrow intolerant spirit of Puritan culture, its lack of "sweetness and light," has been so often insisted on that there is a serious risk of exaggeration.[1] In England, at any rate, some of the most notable representatives of Christian humanism, the Cambridge Platonists, belong to the Puritan tradition and were educated at Emmanuel College, which was the chief center of Puritan influence at Cambridge. The most remarkable of these writers, Peter Sterry, who was one of Oliver Cromwell's chaplains and attended him on his death bed, was also the most humanist of them all. His Platonism is the Christian Platonism of Marsilio Ficino and Pico della Mirandola, who were the real source of the whole movement, but he was also a

[1] H. J. C. Grierson in his *Cross Currents in English Literature in the Seventeenth Century* (1929), ch. vi, "Humanism and the Churches."

man of the widest culture and sympathies, who was a student not only of Plato and Plotinus, but of the medieval schoolmen, the Catholic mystics and of contemporary secular literature, including the dramatists like Shakespeare and Fletcher, who were anathema to the average Puritan.

He writes concerning poetry, "You have examples of this in the Divine pieces of those Divine Spirits, (as they are esteemed and styled) *Homer, Virgil, Tasso,* our English *Spencer,* with some few others like to these; the *Works* of these persons are called *Poems.* So is the Work of God in Creation, and contrivance from the beginning to the end, named ποίημα τοῦ θεοῦ, God's Poem. It is an elegant and judicious Observation of a learned and holy Divine, That the Works of Poets, in the excellencies of their imaginations and contrivances, were imitations drawn from those Original Poems, the Divine works and contrivances of the eternal Spirit. We may by the fairest Lights of Reason and Religion thus judge; That excellent Poets in the heights of their fancies and spirits, were touched and warmed with a Divine Ray, through which the supreme Wisdom formed upon them, and so upon their work, some weak impression and obscure Image of itself."[1]

Thus under the influence of humanism, Christian culture flowered again even on the arid soil of Puritanism. Indeed in the course of the seventeenth century there was a moment when this culture possessed a greater richness of content and a clearer vision of the world *sub specie aeternitatis* than at any time before or since. We see this in England in the writings of Sterry and Traherne and the Christian poetry of Herbert and Vaughan, in France in Yves de Paris, the Franciscan

---

[1] V. de Sola Pinto, *Peter Sterry: Platonist and Puritan* (Cambridge [G.B.], The University Press, 1934), pp. 164–165.

humanist, and throughout Europe in the literature of the great age of Baroque mysticism. It was due, no doubt, to the fact that the men of that age were more conscious than those of any other time that they were heirs of a double tradition and that they all in greater or less degree were at home in two worlds—the world of classical antiquity and the Christian world. They had discovered a new world of knowledge without losing the old world of faith. From the time of Petrarch to that of Milton, the Christian humanists represent the main tradition of Western culture, and their influence still dominated education and literature and art. The secularization of Western culture dates not from the Renaissance or the Reformation but from the Enlightenment of the eighteenth century.

IV. THE INFLUENCE OF SCIENCE
AND TECHNOLOGY

The most striking feature in the educational development which we have surveyed in the last three chapters has been its extraordinary unity. Throughout the whole period from the fourth to the seventeenth century it was dominated consistently by the two great traditions of Christianity and classical culture, and though there were great changes in emphasis and in method and in content, the two basic elements remained constant. The humanists of the Renaissance returned to the sources of the classical tradition, but so had the Carolingian scholars and the thirteenth-century schoolmen. The Reformation was a revolutionary movement which broke the continuity of Western religious tradition, but it also returned to the past and attempted to reform the Church by a restoration of primitive Christianity based on the study of Scripture. At first sight it seems difficult to understand how European culture ever became secularized, since in the seventeenth century both the Baroque culture of the Catholic South and the Protestant culture of the North were inspired by Christian ideals and based on Christian devotion. The universities were still religious corporations, primary and secondary education was still controlled by the clergy, and the literary production of religious works was greater than ever before.

But this is only one side of the picture. Outside the world of books, outside the school and the university, Europe was passing through an immense process of change and a new world was coming into existence. It was a new world in the literal sense, because the age of discovery which began in the fifteenth century had removed the fixed limits of the old *orbis terrarum* and had suddenly opened to Western man a greater world of continents and oceans of which the very existence had been unknown to civilized man. These discoveries were rendered possible by new techniques which had been gradually evolved during the Middle Ages. They belonged to the world of the craftsman and the tradesman rather than to that of the scholar and the scientist, though they were dependent on the latter for the astronomical element in the art of navigation and the use of the astrolabe, the first real scientific instrument which was part of the heritage of Arabic science. For the tradition of Western culture is not confined to the schools; it was also transmitted through the guilds of the craftsmen and the workshops of the artisans. It was here that the new "mechanical" arts were developed which produced those indispensable instruments of Western technology, the clock, the gun and the printing press.

Now in Italy in the age of the Renaissance this tradition of craftsmanship was brought into closer relation with the tradition of higher culture through the medium of art. The artist was the brother of the artisan, and the great Florentine sculptors of the fifteenth century were also craftsmen and goldsmiths, like Verrocchio and Ghiberti and Donatello. The prestige of the artist, which was greater than ever before, communicated itself in some degree to the craftsman and affected every aspect of life and social activity.

So for almost the first time in history we find a highly

cultured and learned society in which manual skill, mechanical technique and scientific and artistic invention were all alike held in high esteem, so that the application of science to life by art and technique became a matter of common concern. The supreme example of this new attitude is to be found in Leonardo da Vinci, who was at once the greatest of Renaissance artists, the greatest master of technical invention and the most original thinker and scientist of his age. Yet Leonardo owed little to formal education, outside Verrocchio's studio. He was proud to call himself *"uomo sanza letere"*—an unlettered man—and he speaks contemptuously of the men of learning who do not use their eyes but only study the ancients. The only true knowledge is to be found in the study of nature and in "the mathematical sciences which contain the truth and the real knowledge of things." This knowledge was applied by Leonardo in every possible field: in painting and sculpture, in architecture and town planning, in engineering and artillery: and he carried his theorizing far beyond the range of contemporary practice into such remote subjects as the mechanical problems of artificial flight.

Yet for all this Leonardo was not an entirely self-taught genius. He inherited a very ancient scientific tradition which had come down to him from Robert Grosseteste and Roger Bacon through the Parisian schoolmen and Nicholas of Cusa to his contemporaries Toscanelli and Luca Pacioli.[1] It was from this source that he derived his idea of experimental science and of mathematics as the universal key that could unlock the secrets of nature. Even his views regarding the practical value

[1] This tradition has been studied in detail by Pierre Duhem in his first important work *Études sur Léonard de Vinci; ceux qu'il a lus et ceux qui l'ont lu.* 3 vols, 1906-9.

of applied science are not new, as they were already expressed by Roger Bacon in the thirteenth century. What is new is the way he unites his scientific theories with the living technical tradition of the Renaissance artist and craftsman. Roger Bacon was a visionary whose experimental science was still not far removed from the magic art of the alchemist and the astrologer. Leonardo was an engineer and a craftsman, and his numerous drawings, like that of the Gun Foundry in the Windsor collection, show how strong was his interest in practical mechanical problems.

But he also differed from his predecessors in a more fundamental sense. The old Oxford tradition of Grosseteste and Roger Bacon was profoundly religious and Christian and mystical, and this is equally true of their fifteenth-century successor Nicholas of Cusa. But while Leonardo da Vinci was far from being irreligious, his religion was in no sense Christian. He was a naturalist and a pantheist in the style of the early Hellenic thinkers. Indeed his aphorisms have a striking resemblance, alike in spirit and form, to those of the pre-Socratic thinkers of Ionia like Heracleitus. "Necessity," he wrote, "is the mistress and guide of Nature; the bridle and the Eternal Law."

This conception of Nature as a living whole governed by its own eternal laws and attaining its own perfection is not peculiar to Leonardo. It is common to the Italian philosophers of the following century—Telesio, Bruno and Campanella, to mention only the most celebrated—but all of them are later than Leonardo da Vinci. Yet in spite of his originality, it is unlikely that it originated with him any more than he originated his theory of experimental science or his theory of mathematics.

What then is its source? It is to be found in his anatomical and biological studies, which brought him into contact with the tradition of medical studies which had their center in the University of Padua. Throughout the later Middle Ages the dominant intellectual influence at Padua had been that of the Averroists, who had separated "scientific" Aristotelianism from theological issues and thus arrived at the dualistic conception of the "two truths" of Reason and Faith, each of them supreme and autonomous in its own sphere. From this paradoxical position it was only a step to thoroughgoing rationalism, and Petrarch has described how frankly the Paduan Averroists of this time professed their contempt for Christianity and their belief in the final authority of reason.[1]

Nothing, of course, is further from Leonardo's philosophy than the scholastic dogmatism of the Averroists, but the latter created an atmosphere of rationalism and scepticism which became widespread in Italy in the fifteenth and sixteenth centuries, especially in the medical faculties of the universities. Moreover the attempt to return to the authentic Greek tradition of Aristotle's teaching, which was carried out by Leonardo's contemporary Pietro Pomponazzi (1462–1525), only strengthened this naturalistic tradition, since his teaching was even more frankly opposed than that of the Averroists to the Christian doctrine of miracles and the immortality of the soul.

Thus while the main tradition of humanist education was Platonic, spiritualist and Christian, the new scientific movement of the Renaissance was sceptical, naturalist and rationalist. And from the time of Pomponazzi onwards this rationalist undercurrent of thought gradually extended from Italy to the rest of Western Europe and especially to France, and influenced the

[1] Its history has been studied in detail by a number of French literary historians: e.g. J. R. Charbonnel, *La Pensée Italienne au XVIe Siècle et le mouvement libertin* (1917) and H. Buisson, *Les Sources et le Développement du Rationalisme dans la Littérature Française de la Renaissance* (1922).

minority who were alienated by the mutual intolerance of the Reformers and their Catholic opponents. Nevertheless it failed to dominate the minds of the leaders of the European scientific movement which came to maturity in the seventeenth century. For the greatest achievements of Renaissance science as represented by Copernicus, Kepler and Galileo were based on the mathematical ideal of natural science which was derived from the medieval tradition of the school of Oxford through Nicholas of Cusa, and ultimately from Plato and Pythagoras rather than from Aristotle and Averroës. And on the other hand, the more the scientists became convinced of the value of the experimental method and the need for exact methods, the more they came to distrust the abstract speculations of the philosophers, orthodox and unorthodox alike. It was not to a representative of traditional orthodoxy, but to Campanella, the disciple of Telesio, that Galileo wrote, "I value the discovery of a truth, even in a small matter, more than disputing at length on the greatest issues without attaining any truth whatever."[1]

But already during Galileo's lifetime the cause of modern science and scientific research was being asserted with unequalled eloquence and conviction by one who was not a mathematician at all. No one today regards Francis Bacon as a great scientist, few consider him a great philosopher, and yet no one did more than he to make the educated world aware of the new power which had been ignored alike by the theologians and the humanists. He was the first man to preach the gospel of the new philosophy of active science with authority and to assert the necessity of a complete reorganization of studies on this new foundation.

In this work of polemic and publicity and propaganda he was

[1] *Galilei opere* (Ed. nat.), IV, 738.

brilliantly successful, and the following generation recognized his unique importance, as we can read in Cowley's famous ode on the foundation of the Royal Society:

> From these and the long Errors of the way,
> In which our wandering Praedecessors went,
> And like th' old *Hebrews* many years did stray
> In Deserts but of small extent,
> *Bacon*, like *Moses*, led us forth at last
> The barren Wilderness he past,
> Did on the very Border stand
> Of the blest promised Land,
> And from the Mountain Tops of his Exalted Wit,
> Saw it himself, and shewed us it.

It is true that Bacon stands outside the main stream of seventeenth-century science, owing to his failure to appreciate the importance of mathematics and the nature of the scientific revolution which was being carried out in the age of Galileo and Huyghens and Newton. On the other hand, he had a clearer conception than any of his contemporaries of the instrumental character of science and its power to transform the conditions of human life. In this he resembles his namesake, Roger Bacon, who had seen experimental science as the instrument by which man could become the master of nature, so that both alike are the precursors and prophets of the technological age. And they also resemble one another in their conception of the relation between science and religion, since both alike believed that there could be no conflict between science and religion, reason and revelation, since both alike tend to the same end—the service and glory of God.

It is true that Francis Bacon's distrust of metaphysics and

mysticism caused him to draw an unnaturally sharp boundary between religion and science which ultimately led to a complete divorce between them. But he could not foresee the use to which Voltaire and the Encyclopaedists would turn his dualism of a fideist theology and an empirical science. He was himself a man of faith, and it is impossible to question the sincerity of the noble prayer which prefaces *Instauratio Magna:*

All depends on keeping the eye steadily fixed upon the facts of nature and so receiving their images simply as they are. For God forbid that we should give out a dream of our own imagination for a pattern of the world; rather may He graciously grant to us to write an apocalypse or true vision of the footsteps of the Creator imprinted on His creatures.

Therefore do Thou, O Father, who gavest the visible light as the first fruits of Creation, and didst breathe into the face of man the intellectual light, as the crown and consummation thereof, guard and protect this work, which coming from Thy Goodness, returneth to Thy Glory. Thou, when Thou turnedest to look upon the works which Thy hands had made, sawest that all was very good and didst rest from Thy labours. But man, when he turned to look upon the work that his hands had made, saw that all was vanity and vexation of spirit and could find no rest therein. Wherefore if we labour in Thy works by the sweat of our brows, Thou wilt make us partakers of Thy Vision and Thy Sabbath. Humbly we pray that this mind may be steadfast in us, and that through these our hands and the hands of others to whom Thou shalt give the same spirit, Thou wilt vouchsafe to endow the human family with new mercies.[1]

This combination of Christian piety with scientific utilitarianism which is so far removed from the Promethean fire of a

[1] Tr. by James Spedding.

Leonardo or a Bruno, was far more acceptable to the mentality of the new bourgeois culture that was developing in England and Holland during the seventeenth century, and it remained characteristic of English scientific thought for more than a century. It was the spirit of the founders of the Royal Society, of Boyle and Sir Isaac Newton and, in a different field, of John Locke. Without any breach with the traditional religious orthodoxy, an intellectual revolution was carried out which transformed the Western conception of the universe and human life and produced far-reaching effects on the tradition of Western education.

The religious conflicts which had divided Western culture for nearly two centuries passed into the background since Protestants and Catholics alike shared the same faith in human nature, the same hope in scientific enlightenment and the same devotion to the cause of humanity and progress.

For though the intellectual movement I have just mentioned was characteristically English and Protestant, the more intellectualist and mathematical tradition of continental thought was carrying out a parallel revolution under the leadership of Descartes. The striking contrast between the mentality and the methods of Descartes and Bacon is apt to make us overlook the similarities between their aims and the work they accomplished. For Descartes no less than Bacon believed in the possibility and the necessity of a complete instauration of learning on a new basis, and he also accepted the utilitarian ideal of science as an instrument of human progress by which men would become "the masters and possessors of nature."

It is true that nothing could be more unlike Bacon's inductive method than Descartes' ideal of a single universal science of pure quantity from which nature could be totally deduced. But both alike made an essential contribution to the development of the modern scientific outlook. And it was the bringing together of these two traditions by the introduction of English ideas into France and the combination of English empiricism with French rationalism that ushered in the Age of Enlightenment.

Throughout the eighteenth century there was an intense interest in scientific ideas which spread through every class of society from the courts to the bourgeoisie and changed the whole climate of European culture. It is true that the traditional forms of education long remained unchanged. Both in England and France the eighteenth century was an age of stagnation in the universities and colleges where the old scholastic methods remained almost unchanged, although they had entirely lost their vitality and their prestige. But outside the walls of the college, everything was being criticized and transformed. Not only were the most revolutionary theories of education being propounded by dozens of writers, but the *instauratio magna* which Bacon had preached had become a living reality—the dominant intellectual force in Western culture.

The basis of this new learning was a mathematical one. Mathematics took the place of scholastic logic and the classics as the fundamental subject, and there has never been an age in which the relations between mathematics and general culture were closer and in which men of letters, like Fontenelle and D'Alembert, made so large a contribution to mathematical studies. As A. N. Whitehead has said so well, "*Les philosophes* were not philosophers. They were men of genius, hard-headed and acute, who applied the seventeenth-century group of scientific abstractions to the analysis of the unbounded universe."[1] These men were superb publicists. They saw clearly and they

---

[1] *Science and the Modern World* (Penguin Ed.), p. 75.

wrote clearly, and whatever they did not see, they ignored. Metaphysics were mere nonsense; religious faith was superstition and mystery was muddle. The age lay wide open to the eye of the philosophic scientist and to the hand of the scientific technologist. All that was necessary was to make men reasonable by education and enlightened government and to free their minds from superstition and prejudice.

Thus the combination of Cartesian rationalism, Newtonian physics and Lockian empiricism produced a highly explosive compound which detonated in the second half of the eighteenth century and almost destroyed the traditional threefold order of Christendom—Church and State and Study. In England, where the Cartesian ingredient was absent, the progress of science had far less revolutionary effects. English Deism was a transitory episode. Science remained faithful to the fideist traditions of Bacon and Newton, and it was in the field of technology that the most important changes took place. In France, on the other hand, science became a philosophy, a creed and a religion. The partisans of the new ideas organized themselves as a militant sect, and under the leadership of D'Alembert, Voltaire and Diderot embarked on one of the most subtle and skillful campaigns of ideological propaganda that has ever been attempted. French was the common language of educated Europe, and wherever French was spoken, or read, in courts and camps, in salons and cafés, from Russia to Portugal, the influence of the sect made itself felt through a thousand different channels.

The great public co-operative work, which had given the movement its name, was the famous Encyclopaedia, edited by Diderot and D'Alembert with the support of the leading French scientists and men of letters, which was published in the midst of many obstacles during the fifteen years from 1750–1765. In spite of all its defects and inadequacies, it was a brilliant success which set its mark on the epoch. It provided the educated world with a *summa* of the new learning—a detailed survey of the whole realm of science and technology and culture, such as had never existed hitherto. Not least important were the sections devoted to technology and industry, which were the work of Diderot, and the excellent series of plates which illustrated them, for they show how men of letters were now fully aware of the coming of the age of the machine and the place of the factory and the workshop in Western culture.

Thus before the industrial revolution had begun, the new philosophy was already preparing the way for its triumph. Science and industry were the two wings of the army of progress which were to be co-ordinated and united by a reformed system of rational education.

Man was born to understand and enjoy Nature, but he was unable to do so as long as his natural instincts were thwarted and his intelligence was twisted and perverted by the unnatural system of education inflicted on him during the most susceptible years of his life. Therefore the first and most essential step in the liberation of humanity is to free the immature mind from the tyranny of priests and pedants. But it was impossible to take this step until the power of the Church, the teaching orders and the universities, had been broken. This was a gigantic task which the philosophers could never have accomplished by their unaided strength. But the old order was divided against itself—the lawyers against the clergy, and the Gallicans against the Ultramontanes, and the Jansenists against the Jesuits—so that the philosophers were able to use their very considerable influence in high places to exploit these internecine feuds. Thus it came about that the Society of Jesus, the greatest of the teaching orders and the chief organ of Catholic culture for two centuries, fell a victim to the intrigues of obscure factions and to the propaganda of the rationalist minority.

Since they had controlled the majority of colleges and secondary schools, not only in France but throughout Catholic Europe, their fall left the whole educational system disorganized and defenceless. But the philosophers were not ready to take advantage of their opportunity. As we see from their correspondence and from D'Alembert's pamphlet "*Sur la destruction des Jésuites en France*," they were taken aback by the suddenness and completeness of their victory. It is true that a number of proposals for reform were put forward, notably by Caradeuc de la Chalotais, one of the leaders of the anti-Jesuit campaign, who advocated a civic and secular system of modern languages and modern scientific studies. Even more significant was the comprehensive plan for a new university composed by Diderot for the Empress Catherine, since this provides the most complete example of the Encyclopaedists' ideal of an advanced scientific education, based on mathematics and including technology as well as physics, biology and chemistry. But little or nothing was done owing to the weakness and apathy of the government. However, throughout the twenty-five years that intervened between the fall of the Jesuits and the French Revolution, the influence of the new ideas continued to spread and the old educational traditions, both of the medieval universities and of the humanist colleges, became more and more discredited.

And so when the revolution came, the old educational institutions found no defenders. The twenty-two universities of France, including the University of Paris, the most famous of all the universities of Europe, fell without a struggle. Their privileges were abolished, their endowments were confiscated, and finally by the law of September, 1793, they were totally suppressed, together with the colleges and most of the surviving secondary schools.[1] Never, not even at the Reformation or the Russian Revolution, was there such a wholesale slaughter of educational institutions. Thus every obstacle was removed which could stand in the way of a complete reorganization of the whole system of national education. Nevertheless the positive achievements of the French Revolution in the sphere of education were small.

Programmes it produced in plenty: the educational programme of Talleyrand in 1791, that of Condorcet in 1792, that sponsored by Robespierre in 1793 and that of Daunou in 1795. All of these programmes are interesting; some, like that of Condorcet, because they anticipate the most advanced ideals for democratic education, others, like the Jacobin programme of 1793, because they foreshadow the worst extravagances of educational totalitarianism; but all of them remained paper schemes, so that by the time Bonaparte attained power France had been without any working system of education for ten years. As Chaptal said when he assumed control, it was a lost generation. One positive achievement, however, can be credited to the Revolution on the technological level; the establishment of the famous Ecole Polytechnique, which was planned by the Committee of Public Safety as a central school of engineering and public works together with the Conservatoire des Arts et Métiers, both of which were to be the pattern for similar institutions throughout the civilized world.

But in spite of these exceptions, it was the task of Bonaparte to rebuild the whole system of national education from its

[1] The only public educational institution which survived was the Collège de France, which still occupies its original site in the Rue des Ecoles.

foundations, and he set about the work in a typically Napoleonic fashion. No one was more conscious of the importance of education for the empire, but his conception of education was a sociological and political one. "Of all political questions," he wrote in 1805, "education is perhaps the most important." "If the child is not taught from infancy to be a republican or a monarchist, a Catholic or a free thinker, and so on, the state will never make a nation. It will rest on shifting and insecure foundations, constantly exposed to disorder and change." "The essential thing is a teaching body, organized on fixed principles like the Jesuits in the past."

But while he had no objection to allowing religious orders like the Brothers of the Christian Schools to establish elementary schools for the lower classes, he had no intention of allowing the Church to recover its old influence on the educational system. On the contrary he was determined to bring the whole system under the direct control of the state, and to make the teaching profession a branch of the civil service. In order to realize this ideal he decreed in 1806 "that there shall be established under the name of the Imperial University, a body exclusively charged with the duty of teaching and public instruction throughout the Empire." This was, of course, not a university in the old sense of the word, since it covered the whole field of education and the whole territory of the Empire. It was a hierarchical authoritarian organization which possessed a complete educational monopoly, for after 1808 it became illegal to establish any school or any establishment of education whatsoever outside the Imperial University and without the authorization of its head, the Grand Master.

Thus by one stroke the new state acquired a total centralized control over education which the Church itself had never possessed in the days when its power was most unchallenged. And though this educational totalitarianism was utterly opposed to the liberal idealism of Talleyrand and Condorcet, it none the less represented the logical conclusion of the Jacobin principle of the civic function of education and of the Encyclopaedist ideal of a unified, rationalized system of national education under secular control. Actually the scheme was too grandiose and the time was too short for it to be fully realized in practice, and private education continued to exist and even to flourish in a modest way. Nevertheless the Napoleonic university marks an epoch in the history of Western education. It stands on the threshold of the new age—an impressive monument to the new power that aspired to control the intellectual life of society and to stamp its mark indelibly on the mind of the individual in the years when it was the most impressionable.

V. NATIONALISM AND THE EDUCATION
OF THE PEOPLE

While the Enlightenment and the Revolution were proceeding triumphantly

> To ruin the great work of Time
> And cast the kingdoms old
> Into another mould

the humbler work of popular education was following an almost independent line of development. As Voltaire wrote, "We have never claimed to enlighten shoemakers and servant girls, they are the portion of the apostles." And in fact, until far on into the nineteenth century the education of the common people was left to the Church or to private religious initiative, since the far-reaching programmes for universal education launched by the French Revolution remained almost entirely without practical effect. Both the Catholic and the Protestant churches had always maintained the principle of the parish school, but this seldom amounted to more than elementary catechetical instruction. In the later seventeenth and early eighteenth centuries, however, both Catholics and Protestants became increasingly aware of their educational responsibilities. In France, St. John Baptist de la Salle founded the institute of the Brothers of the Christian Schools, and in Germany, the

Pietists and the Moravians directed the energies of the Protestant religious revival towards the foundation of orphanages and the development of primary education.

But all these activities belonged to a totally different world from that of the Enlightenment. Indeed there has never been an age in which the religious and the secular worlds were more completely divorced from one another than they were in the eighteenth century. We see this most sharply in France, in the contrast between the educational ideals of the founders of the new orders, like St. John Baptist de la Salle and St. Louis Grignon de Montfort, and those of the Encyclopaedists, and it is hardly less evident in England, where William Law and the Wesleys and the leaders of the Evangelical revival seem to belong to a different culture and a different race of men from those represented by Chesterfield and Gibbon and Horace Walpole.

In Germany also the same contrast exists between the world of the Aufklärung and that of Pietism. But here the contrast was not so sharp, and the gap between these was not too wide to be bridged. This was indirectly due to the lack of political unity and of the centralization of culture which political unity involves. Each of the countless "statelets" of eighteenth-century Germany had its own educational and ecclesiastical organization; many of them had their own universities. These miniature societies were so small that the educated minorities—officials, clergy, professors and teachers—lived in close contact and largely overlapped one another. It was a narrow world still controlled by patriarchal authority and hedged round by restrictions of guild and city and territory and by a rigid medieval class hierarchy which offered few openings to the able and the ambitious. But the effects of this lack of unity were not so unfavorable to culture as we might suppose. As in ancient Greece and

Renaissance Italy the community of culture far transcended the limits of the political society. There was no lack of intercourse between the German states and their cities and universities. A man of ability might find his career in half a dozen different states and feel equally at home in any of them. Germany was in fact a society of states which shared a common culture and a common intellectual life.

In the course of the eighteenth century this almost medieval world of the Holy Roman Empire underwent a movement of change which was hardly less momentous than those which transformed France and England. But in Germany the revolution was not primarily economic or political as in the West, but cultural and educational. Its effects were seen in the world of philosophy and history, music and poetry, and its watchwords were not Liberty and Equality but *Kultur* and *Bildung*. As in France it was stimulated by the Enlightenment, but in Germany the Enlightenment was only the starting point in a voyage of discovery which opened a new world of thought and imagination to the Western mind. The spiritual gulf that separates Voltaire from Goethe, or Condorcet from Herder is so deep that it is hard to realize they were almost contemporaries, and the difference is accentuated by the fact that the temporal rulers of Germany at this time, like Frederick the Great and Joseph II, belonged to the cosmopolitan world of French culture and had no sympathy or understanding for the changes that were taking place in German society.

The intellectual leaders of Germany, on the other hand, were men of humble origin—far more so than in France and England. Winckelmann was the son of an artisan, Kant of a saddler, Herder of a parish clerk, Gauss, the mathematician, of a gardener—all of them came from the people, and though they were highly educated men they could not take their education for granted as the French bourgeois and the English gentleman were accustomed to do. For them education was a social as well as an intellectual problem, and it was to education rather than to politics that they looked for the source of the power that was to transform the world.

Lessing, Kant, Herder, Jean Paul Richter, Fichte and finally Goethe himself all thought long and earnestly about education. Herder began his career in the 1760's with an ambitious plan for the social reform of the Baltic provinces of Latvia by a new system of popular education, and Fichte based his revolutionary programme of German nationalism in 1809 on the principle of compulsory universal national education. No doubt this pre-occupation with education was characteristic of the Enlighten-ment as a European movement, but the Germans were the first to recognize the importance or even the existence of popular culture and vernacular tradition as an independent source of creative activity which deserved the attention of the educa-tionalists no less than the old classical learning of the humanists or the new scientific culture of the French philosophers.

Herder's discovery of the folk song and of primitive poetry as the spontaneous expression of the specific genius of a particular people led him on the one hand to a new appreciation of lan-guage and a new approach to philosophy, and, on the other, to a conception of nationality as the ultimate source of cultural achievement.

This discovery of the value of popular literature and of the importance of the non-rational element in culture led German thought to diverge more and more from the rationalist spirit of the French Enlightenment. It found a natural ally in Rousseau, whose ideas had a profound influence on the German mind. But it was Rousseau the educationalist and the romantic, the author of *Émile* and *La Nouvelle Héloïse*, not Rousseau the political theorist, the author of the *Contrat Social*, who was so important for Germany. Through Herder and Goethe he inspired the German romantic movement; through Kant and Fichte and Schleiermacher he became one of the formative influences of the German philosophical and theological idealism; and finally through Pestalozzi and Froebel his educational ideas first received their practical application.

Pestalozzi, like Rousseau, was Swiss, but his affinities were with German pietism rather than with French rationalism, and there was much in his work that corresponded with the old Christian tradition of education. It is true that his ideas were too novel and revolutionary to gain acceptance in the schools, but they had an extraordinarily wide and stimulating effect on German educational thought and found an echo in the popular literature of the age—in writers like Jean Paul Richter, Johann Heinrich Zschokke and J. P. Hebel. The fact that Jean Paul, the author of the educational romance *Levana*, was at once the disciple of Rousseau, the admirer of Pestalozzi and the favorite author of Metternich shows how the influence of Rousseau, the educationalist, transcended political divisions and became assimilated by German culture.

Nevertheless it was not without its political influence; for the rise of German nationalism in the years of Napoleonic domination was an educational as well as a political movement. In his famous *Address to the German Nation*, Fichte advocated the reform of national education as the indispensable basis of a national revival and pointed to Pestalozzi as the genius who had proved the practicability of the new educational ideals.

In Fichte's view a national education must be universal: it

must concern itself above all with the training of the common people whose education had been neglected or left to the churches in the past. And in the second place it must not be a matter of utilitarian instruction in useful knowledge, but a moral training of the whole man, heart and soul as well as intelligence, for social life and citizenship.

Thus in the German nationalist movement education came before democracy, and political rights were conceived as resulting from the freedom of the mind which was to be won by education.

In fact neither the one nor the other was realized, since the success of the national rising against Napoleon actually resulted in the restoration of the old order and the old territorial principalities. But the nationalist ideal survived, and with it the idea of the new educational ideals which had a much wider diffusion than the political ones. For though Prussia remained the headquarters of the political reaction, it was relatively progressive in educational policy, thanks to the reforms which had been inaugurated by Wilhelm von Humboldt during the years of national revival. Humboldt was himself one of the founders of nineteenth-century liberalism, and he had little sympathy for Fichte's idolization of the national state which makes the latter one of the ancestors of National Socialism. While he shared Fichte's belief in the social mission of education, he conceived this mission in a more universal sense. All learning is one, and it exists not to serve the ends of the state or to train students in their vocational studies but for its own ends, for the disinterested pursuit of knowledge and the development of culture.

Thus the University of Berlin, which was to be the crown of his educational reform, was founded in 1810 not merely as a center of higher education for the nation, but as a center of learning and scientific research which would give an opportunity for the free cultivation of learning for its own sake.

This was one of the decisive moments in the history of European education, for though Humboldt's tenure of the Prussian ministry of Cult and Instruction was brief, his influence and that of the men who were associated with him in the foundation of the University—like Fichte, Schleiermacher, Niebuhr, Savigny and F. A. Wolf—made the new institution a model for the modern universities of Germany and Central and Eastern Europe. And the influence of the Prussian reform of education was hardly less important in the case of the secondary schools, which were reorganized by the Gymnasialordnung of 1812, and the elementary schools, which now for the first time were fully integrated in a complete system of public education.

At first sight it may seem surprising that this progress in national education should have originated in Prussia, the typical example of eighteenth-century bureaucratic absolutism, rather than in France, which had been the leader of the Enlightenment, or England, which was the leader of the movement of technological and industrial progress. But the catastrophe which had overwhelmed Prussia and North Germany had created a political vacuum which allowed the creative forces in German culture, liberated by the literary and philosophic renaissance of the later eighteenth century, to achieve a temporary nation-wide leadership. Although this leadership lasted only half a dozen years, it was sufficient to change the course of history, and its greatest positive achievement was the reform of national education, conceived by Fichte, instituted by Wilhelm von Humboldt and carried out by Suvern.

From the beginnings, however, the work of educational reform was inspired by two different theories or ideologies which were temporarily brought together by the stress of national crisis, but which involved a fundamental contradiction. On the one side there was the liberal humanism of Humboldt, which was inspired by the classical idealism of the Weimar period and transcended political limitations; on the other side, there was the romantic nationalism of Fichte, which regarded education as the moral preparation for citizenship and was prepared to accept the claims of the state as soon as the latter accepted its national mission.

Thus though the German movement began as a liberal revolt against the Napoleonic system, with its bureaucracy, its centralization and its use of education and science as the instruments of the state, it ultimately reached the same ends by a different path. The nineteenth-century nation-state was quick to learn Fichte's lesson that education, above all universal popular education, was the strongest weapon in its armory. All over Europe the progress of liberalism and nationalism was accompanied by the decline in the freedom of the school and the university and the assertion of a state monopoly in education. So long as the state was still a monarchical and absolutist one, as in the years from 1815 to 1848, the universities maintained their independence and sometimes resisted the attempts to repress liberal ideas. But when the state had become identified with the cause of nationalism the case was altered, and nowhere did it find more whole-hearted supporters than among the professors.

This was especially the case in Germany after 1866, where Treitschke, who had begun his career as a liberal, became the enthusiastic supporter of the Bismarckian state and a bitter and intolerant critic of all who opposed it, whether Catholics or

Socialists, Poles or Jews, Saxon and Hanoverian Conservatives or English Liberals.

This is an extreme case, and the learned chauvinism of the professors was perhaps a peculiarly German or Prussian phenomenon. But everywhere in continental Europe during the nineteenth century the reform of the universities and the introduction of a compulsory system of education involved the subordination of education to the ministries of Public Instruction. Everywhere the control of education passed from the Church to the State, and in many countries the rights of the teaching orders to conduct their own schools and colleges were limited or denied. There were, however, two outstanding exceptions to this tendency.

In England and the United States the traditional relation of church and school and the medieval system of corporative independence still survived in spite of the attacks of educational and political reformers. The abuses of the old system and the neglect of primary education were certainly no less flagrant in England than they were on the Continent. But the strength of the voluntary principle and the lack of a centralized authoritarian state caused the reforming movement in England to follow an independent course and to create its own organizations and institutions. The leaders of English thought and action in the decisive years of the eighteenth and nineteenth centuries—the men who created the new industrial and scientific order—like the Arkwrights and George Stevenson, Dalton and Faraday, Huskisson and Cobden, Ricardo and the two Mills, were self-educated men, and the same is true of the founders of the English popular education themselves—Robert Raikes and Joseph Lancaster, J. P. Kay-Shuttleworth and even W. E.

Forster himself, who was responsible for the first Education
Act.

Meanwhile the universities and public schools maintained
their archaic privileges and customs and gradually reformed
themselves under the pressure of public opinion rather than by
direct governmental action. Indeed in the case of Oxford it was
not governmental reform but the resistance to it which produced one of the most influential intellectual movements of
the time. The Oxford Movement was, of course, primarily
religious; nevertheless it had far-reaching effects on education
both in the university and the school. Nor can we ignore its
influence on educational theory, for Newman, the leader of
the Oxford Movement, was also to become the greatest English
Catholic writer on educational theory.

The situation changed after 1870 with the enactment of the
first Education Act and the introduction of universal compulsory education. Henceforward the advance of state control was
slow but continuous, and the English system came more and
more to approximate the continental pattern. The greatest
representative of this tendency was Matthew Arnold, who
spent the whole of his active life from 1865 to 1886 in the service
of the Department of Education as one of H.M. Inspectors of
Schools. As a poet and a humanist he was completely out of
sympathy with the spirit that dominated English public education, and he devoted his great literary abilities to defending
the primacy of spiritual values against the harsh utilitarianism
of the Gradgrind School on the one hand and the narrow sectarianism of the religious denominations on the other. It was a
thankless task to preach "Sweetness and Light" to the managers
of Victorian Board schools. Nevertheless, it was largely due
to his efforts that the ideals of Christian humanism rather than

political nationalism were retained, or at least respected, by the new system of public education which in the course of the following century has gradually overspread and absorbed the whole educational field from the university to the nursery school.

VI. THE DEVELOPMENT OF THE AMERICAN EDUCATIONAL TRADITION

The American tradition of education was originally derived from Great Britain and had little in common with the centralized, state-controlled systems of education which had been characteristic of continental Europe since the eighteenth century. For almost two hundred years it has developed freely on its own lines, so that it has created a new tradition which differs in many respects from either the English or the continental pattern and which has acquired an enormous and increasing influence on the modern world. In order to understand this development it is necessary to study American culture itself, since American education reflects the American way of life, which is the product of many different elements brought together in a new environment and unified at every stage by certain common ideological and institutional influences.

Now we can distinguish four successive periods in the history of American culture, each of which represents the fusion of different elements of population and culture derived from the old world in the new American society. Each of them in turn exercised a formative influence on its successors, and the whole process represents the most elaborate and complex type of culture transmission and formation that is known to us and is available for study. These four periods are:

1. The Colonial period from the early seventeenth century to the Revolution, c. 1607–1774.
2. The period from the Revolution to the Civil War, 1774–1861.
3. The period from the Civil War to the close of unrestricted immigration, 1861–1921.
4. The Contemporary period.

The development of America during the last three of these periods has been more rapid and the changes more far-reaching than in any other known society. They are not merely four periods but four Americas and four American peoples, owing to the geographical and demographic changes in the territory and the composition of the population.

In the first period, it is true, territorial expansion was slow and limited to the Atlantic coastal areas. But even within these areas there were a number of sharply differentiated centers of cultural development. As yet there was no American culture, but rather a number of colonial provincial cultures which possessed different religious traditions and tended to group themselves round a Northern focus in New England and a Southern focus in Virginia, while the middle colonies from Pennsylvania to New York developed somewhat later and possessed a more varied background.

Throughout the colonial period the educational tradition was predominantly English and was differentiated chiefly by its religious and ecclesiastical affiliation. In Puritan New England public interest in education was always exceptionally strong, and the school from the beginning formed one of the essential organs of the New England town or village community. Here also the institutions for higher education, like the colleges of

Harvard and Yale, were old and flourishing, but these, even more than the English universities, were primarily clerical institutions. Even as late as 1752 the President of Yale defined their function in thoroughly traditional and even medieval terms. "Colleges," he wrote, "are *Religious Societies* of a Superior Nature to all others. For whereas *Parishes* are societies for training up the *Common People*, Colleges are *Societies of Ministers*, for training up Persons for the Work of the Ministry."[1]

In the South, in the predominantly Anglican colonies, education was far less developed, partly owing to the pattern of settlement and economic life, but also to the neglect of their colonial responsibilities by the Church of England. It was not until the eighteenth century with the Society of the Propagation of the Gospel (SPG) that the Anglicans began to take their responsibilities seriously, especially in the Middle and Northern colonies, but the foundation of Kings College in New York, the most important Anglican center of higher education, came too late (1754) to have a deep influence on American culture. For the age of the Revolution had a disastrous effect on the Anglican Church in America, owing to its association with the King's government and the loyalist sympathies of the majority of the clergy.

The ideology of the Founding Fathers was that of the Enlightenment, and their educational ideas, as represented above all by Franklin and Jefferson, were strongly influenced by the theories of contemporary French philosophy. It is true that the enlightened and far-reaching plans of Jefferson for a system of

[1] Thomas Clap, *The Religious Constitution of Colleges, especially of Yale College in New Haven, 1754.* Quoted in R. Freeman Butts and Lawrence A. Cremin, *History of Education in American Culture* (New York, Holt, 1953).

national education produced no immediate result, owing to the extreme individualism of early American society, the weakness of both the federal and state governments and the profound social changes due to the rapid expansion of Western settlement. But the general effect of the Revolution and the new democratic ideology produced a widespread interest in and demand for popular education, which was to bear fruit in the nineteenth century.

The period from the Revolution to the Civil War was the great creative age of American culture. It saw the fusion of the colonial cultures in a new American national unity, but at the same time an enormous territorial expansion transformed the geographical character of the country and a vast movement of internal colonization transformed the sociological structure of the population. The dynamic element in this movement was not the new immigration from Europe, which only reached mass proportions in the middle of the nineteenth century, but rather the immigrants of the late colonial period, above all the Irish Presbyterians—the so-called "Scotch-Irish"—who produced such typical personalities as Jackson and Calhoun. It is difficult to exaggerate the importance of this element, since it is not confined to a single section like the older Puritan immigration to New England, but was common to the North and the South, being especially important in New Hampshire and western New York, in Pennsylvania and West Virginia, and in North Carolina and Georgia.

In some respects this migration may be compared with the earlier Puritan immigration, as it was also partly due to religious motives and the spirit of Irish Presbyterianism was no less intransigent and militant than that of English Puritanism. In fact the great migration of the middle decades of the eighteenth century must be regarded as the third element (after the Virginian settlement and the Puritan migration to New England) in the formation of the American people. Indeed many of the features in American culture, especially in the second period, which are usually attributed to the influence of the Puritan tradition of New England are really due to the Presbyterian tradition of this later Irish (and especially though not exclusively Ulster) migration. Moreover it was owing to the predominance of this element in the newly settled areas that the Anglicanism of the original Virginia society failed to establish itself further inland, and even tended to wither away in eastern Virginia itself.

All these three elements intermingled with one another in the new lands between the Alleghenies and the Mississippi and formed a new people. The process began early in the eighteenth century and reached its climax in the 1830's, when the new America attained its majority in the presidency of Andrew Jackson. It was not a process of systematic group settlement as in the old colonial period, but of rapid, continuous and kaleidoscopic change, as we see in the case of Abraham Lincoln's family, which moved in four or five generations from New England to Pennsylvania, from Pennsylvania to Virginia, from Virginia to Kentucky, back to Virginia and on to Indiana and Illinois.

The history of the whole period is conditioned by this restless urge to territorial expansion which was largely responsible for the War of 1812, the war with Mexico and the countless Indian wars. Indeed it was a warlike period, beginning and ending in two great wars, each of which lasted for years and changed the whole course of history and social life in North

America. It was also a period of great political experiment and change, an age of constitution-making and of the creation of the American tradition of jurisprudence. Indeed it was the lawyers and the philosophers of law who were the leading element in American culture at that period, to an extent which can hardly be paralleled elsewhere. The leading political figures of that period, after Washington, were all lawyers, like Webster and Henry Clay and Calhoun. Even Jackson himself was a lawyer as well as a soldier and a politician.

This feature is common to North and South and West, but it was in Virginia that the tradition of legal culture was strongest, and throughout the earlier part of the period Virginia retained its political leadership. Of the first twelve presidents of the United States down to 1850, six came from Virginia and two from Tennessee, as against two from New England and one from New York.[1] Thus the influence of the South was far stronger in the first half of the nineteenth century than at any later period, and this was also the case in the West, where the settlement of Kentucky and Tennessee preceded that of the North West.

It is true that New England was always in advance of the South in education and literary culture. But this meant that New England was more closely in touch with Europe and more dependent on Old World standards of culture. But in the new lands beyond the Alleghenies Europe was very far away. Men looked west to the Mississippi and beyond to the boundless virgin spaces of an empty continent. It is difficult for us to imagine what life was like at Knoxville or Lexington at the end

[1] Reckoning W. H. Harrison as a Virginian for family reasons, though he had settled in Ohio; one might add Taylor also as a Virginian by birth.

of the eighteenth century, considering the sparse population and the vast distance that separated them from the old centers of population. Yet these were state capitals, where the constitutions of the first Western states were established, and it was from this remote, and in many respects primitive, world that the leading figures of the age—men like Jackson, Polk, Henry Clay and Lincoln—emerged.

The American religious and cultural tradition underwent great changes in the new environment. The older churches, like the Congregationalism of New England and the Anglicanism of Virginia, failed to establish themselves. The latter had been almost ruined by the Revolution, and its place was taken by new sects like the Separatist Baptist churches which established themselves in North Carolina and Georgia just before the Revolution and spread with great rapidity throughout the South. At the same time the Methodist movement reached America and soon spread into the West, and there were also new forms of Presbyterianism like the Cumberland Presbyterians and the Disciples of Christ.

This new type of Western American Protestantism was often accompanied by extreme forms of mass excitement and revivalism such as marked the great religious awakening that swept Kentucky and the West at the beginning of the nineteenth century. At the same time it was the religious denominations rather than the state that were the chief organs of culture and education in the West, and the new colleges which arose like mushrooms in the Western territories usually owed their foundation to some church or to religious societies like the Society for the Promotion of Collegiate and Theological Education in the West, and these were inspired by precisely the same principles as those formulated by the President of Yale a century earlier.[1]

Meanwhile in the East, and above all in New England, the state governments became increasingly aware of their educational responsibilities and gradually evolved an efficient and universal system of public education. The great organizer and propagandist of the movement in Massachusetts, Horace Mann (1796–1859) was deeply influenced by his visits to Europe, and especially by what he saw of the Prussian system of national education and teacher training and by the ideal of the German educational reformers. The same tendencies were represented by Henry Barnard in Connecticut and were reinforced by the admiration of the New England Transcendentalists in the '40's for German philosophic ideas. In the second half of the nineteenth century the influence of the Swiss and German educational reformers—Pestalozzi, Froebel and Herbart—became increasingly strong in America, and at the same time higher education in the leading American universities began to follow the German pattern of specialization and research, with a growing emphasis on the importance of post-graduate study.

Thus American education, which had originally been based on a close bond between church and school and a minimum of state control, after the old English tradition, became reorganized in the later nineteenth century and early twentieth century on continental, and especially German, lines. The men who founded or refounded modern American education, like Horace Mann, were hostile to the denominational principle and in favor of state control and public support.

[1] The Report of this society for 1840 writes: "The *Ministry* is God's instrumentality for the conversion of the World. Colleges and Seminaries are God's means of training up a learned and efficient *Ministry*." Quoted in Butts and Cremin, *op. cit.*, p. 200.

There was no anti-clerical propaganda against religious teaching and no limitation on the freedom of independent schools and colleges, as on the European continent, but there has been a steady tendency towards the extension of public control and to the secularization of teaching, so that the American common school and high school which educate the vast majority of the American people base their teaching on democratic moral values and the ideals of national patriotism rather than on any religious doctrine or ethos.

This development was a natural consequence of the social and intellectual changes that followed the Civil War. The new America that emerged from the war was infinitely richer and stronger and more successful than the America of the early nineteenth century. The material achievement of the period from the Civil War to the first World War surpassed the most sanguine forecasts of the earlier period. It saw the population increasing from thirty-one millions to over a hundred millions and wealth increasing still more rapidly. It saw the whole continental area from the Atlantic to the Pacific settled, organized into states and united in an advanced industrial economy. It was the golden age of American capitalism and the iron age of American industrialism: the age of the great constructive enterprises, the great trusts and the great monopolies.

At the same time it saw profound changes in the character and composition of the American people. In the Civil War the Americans were still a rural people. At the end of the period the United States had the largest urban population in the world, and the fact that the American cities were so new made them more uniform, so that to the outsider it seemed that there was one great American city which reproduced itself endlessly. And whereas the old American city was extremely provincial and close to the soil, the new American city was exceedingly cosmopolitan owing to the fact that it drew its population from every part of Europe and America. For this was the great age of foreign immigration, and from the Civil War to the First World War practically every people in Europe sent a continuous stream of new citizens to populate the new cities, and to a lesser degree the newly opened farm lands of the Middle and North West.

This flood of foreign immigration had already begun by the middle of the nineteenth century, when the great Irish migration took place, but it did not reach its peak till the beginning of the twentieth century, when the vast influx of Italians and Poles and Russians and Czechs and Slovaks and Hungarians came surging across the Atlantic. By this time the earlier immigrants, especially the Irish, had become Americanized, so that they held a somewhat similar position in the third period to that which the Irish Protestant immigrants had played during the second. But these two earlier elements were, after all, akin, even though they were divided by religious and political antagonisms. It is true that the Irish Catholic population had little effect on the intellectual life of the American people. Even if they had had more to give, their religious separation from the majority would have prevented their communicating it. But they had a very great importance for the social life, since their advent coincided with that of the new cities and of American urban life; and since they were predominantly a city population, they came in, as we say, on the ground floor.

In any case the importance of this age was not intellectual. There were few great writers, and what there were were mostly survivors from the previous age, like Emerson and Oliver Wendell Holmes, or expatriates like Henry James. On the other hand, it was a great age for education, and both the American common school and the American university acquired a new form and extension at this time. It was, I think, in this period that school and college took the place of church as the cultural center of American life. The materialism of that age was unfavorable to the type of religious idealism that had created the new American forms of sectarian Protestantism, and the change that passed over the Mormons—from millenniarist fanaticism to practical business organization—was a typical one. But economic materialism did not hinder the growth of education. Indeed one of the main outlets for the new wealth was found in the endowment of colleges and universities. Further, the development of education and educational institutions was a potent influence in the unification of American culture at a time when territorial expansion and foreign immigration both alike tended to make for disintegration.

At the same time the new faith in science which took the place of theological orthodoxy only strengthened American faith in the possibilities of democratic education. If science is destined to rule and transform the world, education is the means by which science is socialized and made universal. This was most clearly seen by Lester Ward, the sociologist (1841–1913), who differs from most of his contemporaries in having spent his life not in business or education but in the service of the federal government as a geologist and statistician. He consequently took a much more favorable attitude towards socialization and governmental action than was usual in his time. In his view the great problem on which all else depended was the utilization of the intellectual potentiality of society by a scientific system of universal education. "The great demand of the world is knowledge. The great problem is the equalization of intelligence, to put all knowledge in the possession of every human being. Intelligence, heretofore a growth, is destined to become a manufacture.... The origination and distribution of knowledge can no longer be left to chance and nature."[1] And in the same way democratic government can no longer be left to amateur politicians, it must become a scientific activity. Every legislature must become a laboratory of sociological research, and every legislator must become a sociologist.

Ward's theories of education and government seem to point towards a totalitarian technology which is very alien from the American tradition. Yet the same tendencies towards social-ization and secularism are to be found in the teaching of John Dewey, who was perhaps the most influential of all modern American educationalists. In his views the purpose of education is not the communication of knowledge but the sharing of social experience, so that the child shall become integrated into the democratic community. He believed that morals were essentially social and pragmatic and that any attempt to sub-ordinate education to transcendent values or dogmas ought to be resisted. Lester Ward had seen education as the great social panacea in the hands of a scientific authority, but to Dewey it was rather a humanitarian religion, the pastoral ministry of the democratic community.

At the same time Dewey represents only one side of this tradition. He stands for the socialization of education to such a degree that there is a real danger of the school becoming an instrument of social conformity and a means for the establish-ment of the mass mind, or as he puts it, "the pooled intelligence" of the democratic mind.

[1] Quoted in Henry S. Commager, *The American Mind* (New Haven, Yale University Press, 1950), pp. 213-14.

But this educational ideal is in contradiction with the element of spiritual individualism which is equally a part of the educational tradition of Rousseau. In this respect Dewey represents the opposite pole of American thought from Thoreau, who was also a disciple of Rousseau and was also deeply concerned with the problem of democratic education, but who was averse to any suggestion of state control and conceived of education in the traditional way as the initiation of the mind into the tradition of higher culture as represented by the classical literatures of the past, not as the initiation of the child into the technology and politics of contemporary society.[1]

But however great is the gulf that separates Ward and Dewey from Thoreau, they are in agreement on one essential point— that a really democratic education involves higher education for all and not only for a privileged class. And this principle has been realized to a greater extent in the United States than anywhere else in the world. The Greek ideal of the Good Life as the birthright of the citizen has been extended from a limited citizen class to the whole population. No doubt the American version of this ideal and the corresponding educational practice would be criticized by Aristotle as banausic, but Aristotle belonged to the pre-technological age and the modern conditions make it inevitable that higher education should be orientated towards technology and vocational studies rather than philosophy and contemplation. At the present time any democratic

[1] "We are underbred and low lived and illiterate; and in this respect I do not make any very broad distinction between the illiterateness of my townsmen who cannot read at all and the illiterateness of him who has learned to read only what is good for children and feeble intellects. We should be as good as the worthies of antiquity, but partly by first knowing how good they were. We are a race of tit-men, and soar but little higher in our intellectual flights than the columns of the daily paper." *The Works of Henry D. Thoreau* (New York, Crowell, 1940), p. 141.

system of education must conform to the economic and practical needs of democratic society rather than to the old ideals
of scholarship, and the American form of democratic education
is the most universal and the most encompassing that the world
has ever seen. It accepts everyone, and it teaches everything
from Chinese to chiropody. It numbers its universities by the
hundred, its high schools by the thousand, and its students by
the million, and it is growing all the time at breathless speed.

   This vast expansion of American education did not, of course,
take place until the present age, during the fourth of the periods
into which I have divided the development of American culture.
No doubt there is some difference of opinion as to when this
new age began. Some would date it from the First World War,
others from the great economic depression of 1929, but I believe
that the real turning point came with the ending of the period
of unrestricted immigration in 1921, for this marks a significant
change in the world position of the United States, from the
open door from the Old to the New World into the largest
and most powerful nationality of the Western world as a whole.
The United States had now become a relatively centralized
national state with a much higher degree of cultural uniformity
than many of the states of the Old World. Yet it was far less
unified in population than in the past. It had become one of the
most cosmopolitan populations in the world, and contained at
the beginning of this period large blocks of non-English- speaking population. There is an apparent contradiction between this
racial and linguistic diversity and the uniformity of American
culture, and this has accentuated the tendency of American
nationality to be more conscious and more "cerebral" than in
the nations of the Old World. For the son of the Italian or
Polish Jewish immigrant in New York was no less "American"

than the highland farmer in West Virginia; in a sense he was more American, more representative and more integrated into the new American culture, whereas the other was a survivor from an America that no longer existed.

This new cosmopolitan urban national culture was the great reality of the fourth period. In comparison with it, all the older strata of American society had acquired a kind of mythical character. And it is characteristic of the American development that even the recent past becomes enveloped in an aura of romantic legend. There is the legend of the South, the legend of New England, the legend of the West—of the covered wagon and the cowboy. And in this fourth period all these legends became canonized and popularized in the great national myth-factories of Hollywood.

It was in this period that the urban element in American culture attained its full development with a corresponding decline of rural life. The change in social habits was even greater than in Europe during the Industrial Revolution, because the American city was such a recent development and it had had to improvise its new ways of life; yet they were more advanced from a mechanical point of view than anything to be found in Europe, and also more fluid. The effects on American culture and society have been studied recently by a number of sociologists such as David Riesman, who has described how the type of social "character which dominated America in the nineteenth century had gradually been replaced by a social character of quite a different kind."

The great problem of the present age is whether the new structure of American society can continue to develop in this way, like a sociological skyscraper, without becoming so divorced from its agrarian foundations that the latter become physically exhausted and spiritually depressed by the structure they have to bear. For it is an abnormally expensive economy which uses up both human and natural resources more rapidly than anything hitherto known. Yet even in the past we see how the relatively simple urban development of the Mediterranean world proved too expensive for the peasant economy of those lands to maintain it indefinitely.

The new American culture has attempted and largely achieved something that has never been regarded as within the range of possibility—luxury for all. No doubt there are still backward areas and underprivileged classes and sections, particularly the Negroes. Nevertheless these are the exceptions, whereas in the past they have been the rule. But the result of this is that America, which was originally the land of equality, has become a privileged society, a kind of world aristocracy. No doubt a hundred years ago the American farmer and frontiersman had a far higher standard of life than the Chinese peasant or coolie. But then there was no comparison—there were two separate worlds—whereas today everyone in Asia and even in Africa is aware of the American way of life as a standard which they cannot attain and against which they feel a certain resentment in consequence.

These external repercussions of American culture on the Old World are generally recognized today and great efforts are being made to deal with them, but this inevitably involves an increasing pressure, both economic and moral, on the American system. This burden of world responsibility is a new factor in American life, and it is a source of internal strain, since it runs counter to the old tradition of autonomy and autarky and freedom from the guilt of history—the original sin of the Old

World—which has always been the dominant spirit of American culture.

There are other tendencies in the new state of culture which are in conflict with the old American tradition, for example the high degree of professional specialization, which is inevitable in a scientific technological order, conflicts with the older tradition by which the American was ready to turn his hand to everything and was not tied down to a particular profession from the beginning, and still more the bureaucratic centralized system of the urbanized mass state seems hard to reconcile with the American tradition of government and the pattern of democratic individualism.

But there are other factors to be taken into account which must affect the character of American culture in the future. In the first place, the last period has been marked by an immense advance in education, including higher education, so that for the first time in history the ideal of higher education for all citizens is within the range of possibility. This must affect the character of the mass society, for in the past a mass society has always been considered a society of illiterate masses. A highly educated mass society is a new experiment, and even if the general quality of the education is not high, it is capable of progressive improvement and provides new standards of intellectual value and opportunities for self-criticism which were lacking in the earlier forms of American democracy.

Moreover owing to the economic resources of the system, and the generosity of the giant capitalist funds for educational purposes, such as the Rockefeller Foundation, and the co-operative programmes for the international exchange of scholars and students, American education is becoming a world-wide force and is bound to influence the new systems of public education which are being created in Asia and Africa by the new national states. Here the only effective rival to the American system is that of the Communist states, which are equally convinced of the importance of education for all and of the necessity for making the university a training ground for experts who will be capable of running the complex mechanism of modern industrial and technological society. The difference between the two systems consists in the fact that Communist education is based on a single authoritative state ideology and allows little or no scope for academic freedom, whereas in America the government does not yet claim an academic monopoly and the principle of academic freedom is still accepted in theory, though it may be limited in practice by the pressure of public opinion and by the desire to make the school an organ of national and democratic integration.

In the past in America, as also in England, educational freedom was due in large measure to the dual origin of the system; to the fact that the churches possessed their own schools and colleges under their own control alongside of the free secular public schools and colleges which were maintained and controlled by the state. During the last fifty years the importance of the former has indeed diminished, so that with one exception the American educational system has been tending towards uniformity. But this exception is an important one, for the Catholics of the United States, who now number more than forty millions, possess their own independent educational institutions embracing the whole educational curriculum from the elementary school to the university.

VII. CATHOLIC EDUCATION AND CULTURE IN AMERICA

We have seen how the American educational system represents the culmination of the age-long development of Western education which has now become universal in scope and world-wide in its influence. It rivals the educational system of the Soviet Union in offering scientific and technological instruction to the members of the new nationalities and of the more backward cultures from Indonesia to West Africa, and therefore may be seen as an indispensable instrument for the creation of a free world. But in one important respect it has departed from its Western origins and has become similar to its Communist and totalitarian rival. As in Russia it has become almost completely secularized and leaves little place for those religious studies which were the original *raison d'être* of the Western university. The separation of Church and State which was originally a purely political measure has been extended to the educational field and has resulted in the exclusion of religion from the domain of public education.

Nevertheless, as I mentioned in the last chapter, the principle of freedom of education is deeply rooted in the American tradition, and this has enabled the religious minorities to maintain their own educational institutions alongside of the public schools and the state universities. As a rule the independent

Protestant schools and colleges have gradually conformed to the secular pattern of modern American education. But in the case of the Catholics this is not so. In the course of time they have created an independent educational system extending from the primary school to the university and covering the whole of the United States with the exception of the so-called "Bible Belt" in the deep South, where the whole population remains solidly Protestant.

The building up of this independent educational system is an essential part of the growth of that new American Catholicism which is such a characteristic feature of modern America. What makes this development so paradoxical is that it is, so to speak, the by-product of the social and political expansion of Protestantism in the New World, so that today the influence of the Catholicism of Protestant America has come to outweigh in importance the Catholicism of Catholic America. From the beginning, from the time when Columbus landed in the Bahamas, the Catholic Church has played a leading part in the discovery and settlement of America, not only in South America but in the north also—from Florida to California and from the mouth of the Mississippi to the Great Lakes.

But all these centuries of effort and missionary achievement did not create the American Church that we know. The conquerors and the explorers, the missionaries and the converts, represent one side of the Catholic history in the New World, but it is the other side that is responsible for everything that we think of as American Catholicism, and that side is represented by the church of the Catholic immigrants who entered the purely Protestant culture of the English colonies and the states that were their successors, gradually creating a diaspora, a network of Catholic minorities throughout the whole of the

United States. This movement extended with the western advance of the American nation and, as it advanced, it incorporated and swallowed up the older Catholic communities which owed their existence to the other earlier movements of French and Spanish origin.

The one exception to this process was the little colonial Anglo-American Church of Maryland. Its numbers were never large, and throughout the colonial period its existence depended entirely on the ministry of the Jesuits of the English province, of whom some 185 came to America in the first 140 years of Maryland's existence. But its importance is out of proportion to its size, since it provides a vital historical link with the native English tradition of Catholicism and with the native American tradition of English culture, and at the time of the Revolution it gave Catholics a modest share in the foundation of the United States through the participation of some of its representatives, like the Carrolls.

Apart from this narrow thread of historical continuity with the English colonial past, American Catholicism owes everything—even its existence—to the immigrants—first to the French who left Europe and the West Indies at the time of the Revolution, then to the Irish and the Germans and finally to the Poles and Italians and Czechs and Hungarians and Ukrainians who continued to swell the tide of foreign migration down to the age of the world wars.

Of all these elements, it was the Irish that were the most important from the religious and social point of view. In spite of their intense loyalty to Ireland and to one another, they were the element that adapted itself most rapidly and completely to the American way of life, and they brought with them from their native land that tradition of solidarity between priest and people which has been the common characteristic of American and Irish Catholicism.

Many of the features in American Catholicism which distinguish it from continental European Catholicism are really as much Irish as they are American. In Europe there was, generally speaking, an alliance between the Church and the Catholic State, and between the clergy and the conservative ruling class. But the Irish immigrants had brought with them from the old country a profound distrust of the Protestant government and usually an open hostility to it. And on the other hand there was a close social alliance between the common people and their priests, who were of the same blood and class and culture and who had taken the place of the ruling class as the social leaders of the people. Thus the democratic character of American Catholicism, which is the first thing that strikes the foreign observer, is not entirely a product of American conditions, but owes its basic character to its Irish inheritance.

It is true that this Irish tradition underwent a profound change in America. It lost its native language and with it the rich inheritance of Gaelic peasant culture. But this was the necessary price that they had to pay for their successful adaptation to American society, since the fact that they were English-speaking gave them a great advantage over all the other immigrant groups. At the same time they transformed themselves from a peasant class into an urban proletariat, and they did it so thoroughly that in the course of the nineteenth century they became the predominant element in most of the great American cities. By carrying out this revolutionary process of social transformation, the Irish created the new social pattern of urban Catholicism which was adopted by almost all the subsequent immigrant groups with the exception of the Germans. These later immigrants—Poles, Italians, Czechs, Hungarians, Lithuanians and Ukrainians—were, like the Irish, uprooted peasants who became city dwellers in the New World and who found in the life of their Catholic churches and parishes and schools the moral protection and the element of spiritual community which enabled them to survive in their new environment.

This is perhaps the most important factor which distinguishes the social tradition of American Catholicism from that of the Old World. In Europe it was the peasants who remained most loyal to the Church and who probably provided the greatest number of religious vocations, while in the great cities the Church had to face the growing opposition of the forces of anti-clericalism and irreligion. But in America the situation was just the opposite. The whole strength of the Church lay in the cities—especially the great cities of the East and the Middle West, while the rural districts, apart from the areas of German settlement in northern Ohio and elsewhere, were solidly Protestant, and in many cases maintained all the anti-Catholic prejudices and delusions of the past. This situation was all the more significant because the earlier American culture was predominantly a rural one. When the movement of Catholic immigration started, the American urban civilization did not exist. American Catholicism has grown up with the American cities and their civilization, so that the place of Catholicism in modern American culture, which is now an urban one, is even more important than its numbers and its date of origin would lead one to suppose.

In spite of this, throughout the nineteenth century, and indeed down to the age of the world wars, the social prestige and the cultural achievements of American Catholics were very modest. Catholics were an underprivileged, disregarded minority, and the Catholic Church was the church of the poor and the strangers. All through the middle decades of the century, Catholics were exposed to a campaign of misrepresentation and abuse, which sometimes, as in Boston and Philadelphia, reached the pitch of open persecution and the burning of churches and convents. Yet in spite of it, the progress of American Catholicism went on without a break. Unpopularity and lack of privilege may have been unfavorable to the development of an intellectual culture, but they strengthened the social solidarity of the Church and the loyalty of the Catholic people to their religious leaders. In the midst of economic hardship American Catholics built up their own social and educational institutions until the Catholic Church became the most highly organized and well-equipped religious body in the United States.

Under these circumstances it would be unreasonable to reproach American Catholicism for not producing scholars and philosophers and men of letters. It was the church of the poor, and the starving Irish peasants who fled from the famine or the uneducated peasants from Central Europe who came to America to work in the mines and factories could not hand on a tradition of Catholic intellectual culture that they had never possessed. Everything had to be built up from the foundations, and the present state of Catholicism in the United States is a proof of the greatness of their effort and the solidity of their achievement. By the end of the nineteenth century, under the leadership of Cardinal Gibbons, American Catholicism had established its position securely as an integral element in the life of the nation, and American Catholics were becoming increasingly aware of their strength and of the new opportunities which were being opened to Catholicism by the civilization of the New World.

Hence the spiritual and intellectual leaders of American Catholicism—men like Father Hecker, the founder of the Paulists, John Ireland, the famous Archbishop of St. Paul, and Bishop Keane, the first rector of Catholic University—were foremost in the advocacy of American ideals and the defense of the American way of life. They held that the freedom of Anglo-Saxon institutions was in practice more favorable to the progress of Catholicism than the outmoded patterns of the European Catholic state and that the democratic Catholicism of the New World was destined to be the Catholicism of the new age. But this optimism proved to be somewhat premature. It provoked a controversy between conservative and liberal Catholics both in America and Europe which resulted in Leo XIII's letter to Cardinal Gibbons condemning "opinions which some comprise under the name of Americanism," with special reference to Elliot's life of Father Hecker, which had been the center of the controversy, especially in France.

It was a strange and inconclusive controversy, since the Americanists of America, as represented by Archbishop Ireland, denied that such opinions had ever existed among them, and the Americanists of France, like Abbé Klein, described Americanism as a theological phantom. The confusion arose from the fact that the Americanists were no theologians and the anti-Americanists knew very little about America. The fact was that a new Catholic society and way of life had emerged as an integral part of the great new American democratic civilization, sharing the same characteristics, the same weakness and the same strength. It was a living reality, not a theory. Where its critics and admirers both went wrong was in attributing to it an ideology that it did not possess. For there was in fact no such thing as Americanism: there were only American Catholics. It was not until ten or twenty years after the Americanist controversy was over that American Catholicism began to acquire full cultural consciousness.

For it was only after the closing down of European immigration after the first World War that the barriers which separated the immigrants from the native American were overcome and real social and cultural unity between the two elements in the population was finally achieved. The results of this have become increasingly visible since the end of the Second World War, and they find expression in three different directions.

First, the Catholics have ceased to be regarded as Irish Americans or as Polish Americans, and have become simply American Catholics—and this was just what Cardinal Gibbons and so many of the Catholic leaders of the past had been aiming at. Secondly, Catholics have gained a new economic and social status. They are no longer an underprivileged proletariat, as they were more or less throughout the nineteenth century, and have become largely a middle-class community. This involves a certain loss, since the fact that the American Church was predominantly the church of the poor was a source of spiritual strength from the religious point of view. But seen in relation to American culture, the achievement of economic success is such an important source of social prestige that it was difficult for Catholics to take their full share in American life without it. And thirdly, the last twenty years has seen a great advance in Catholic education and a growing awareness of the importance of intellectual values and of the need for a Catholic culture.

This was the greatest weakness of American Catholicism in the past, owing largely to the lack of economic opportunity and to the lack of any cultural tradition among most of the immigrant groups: and even today it is commonly said that Catholics do not take their proportionate share in the intellectual life of the nation. But against this we must set the remarkable achievements of American Catholic education—3,500,000 children in elementary schools, 700,000 secondary school pupils, and 300,000 students in universities and colleges—a record of voluntary effort which I believe has no parallel elsewhere in the world.

No doubt the results on the level of higher intellectual culture are disappointing, but so they are in American secular education, where the vast expenditures of money and effort over the last thirty years have not produced a corresponding advance of higher culture. But the creation of this massive educational system is in itself a great achievement and may have an even greater importance for the future. For as education reaches a certain point of development, it opens up new and wider cultural horizons. It ceases to be a utilitarian parochial effort for the maintenance of a minimum standard of religious instruction and becomes the gateway to the wider kingdom of Catholic culture which has two thousand years of tradition behind it and is literally world-wide in its extent and scope.

In the past, owing to adverse circumstances, American Catholics were deprived of this cultural heritage and forced to exist as outsiders on the periphery of a dominant Protestant culture. Nevertheless they were the legitimate heirs of a much richer cultural inheritance than anything that American Protestantism knew, and now that they are free to enter into their inheritance, they will ultimately be able to exert an increasing influence on American thought and culture. It is obvious that this is an infinitely more important issue than the questions of political influence, questions which have a certain journalistic appeal but which only touch the surface of Catholic life.

It is the cultural issue that is the vital one, for it is only by a communication of culture and the meeting of minds that it is possible to make Americans realize the true nature of Catholicism and the real significance of Catholic values. Throughout the greater part of the nineteenth century it is safe to say that American Protestants knew less than nothing about all this. What they thought they knew was a caricature—a stereotype imposed by centuries of religious controversy and prejudice. And even today this state of ignorance is by no means fully dissipated.

Now it is easy to explain the misunderstandings which inspired the Know Nothing movement a century ago. The New Englanders, for instance, had their own highly developed regional culture, based on the old Puritan tradition and the new Unitarian ideology, and it was natural that they should resent the incursion of vast hordes of uneducated Catholics, speaking what was almost a strange language and worshipping, so to speak, strange gods.

But all this is ancient history. The descendants of the immigrants today are as American as the descendants of the Pilgrim Fathers, and the modern American Catholics are an educated people who have learned to adapt themselves to the American way of life without sacrificing their own religious and intellectual traditions. It is true, Catholics are still a minority in a traditionally Protestant culture, but they are a very strong minority—far larger and stronger and better organized than many of the Catholic majorities in the Old World.

In the past, as we have said, Catholic higher education in America was relatively unimportant and the main effort of the Church was concentrated on the elementary needs of the parochial school. It is only in the present century—and even in the present generation—that Catholics have been able to devote their attention to the university and have thus become capable of making their own distinctive contribution to American culture.

The nature of their contribution is obvious. For the Catholic colleges stand alone—or almost alone—as the representatives of the age-long tradition of Christian education in the United States. It has always been the curse of education that it has been under the spell of the past in its methods and ideas. But today this past is not the past of the medieval schoolmen or the Renaissance humanists; it is the late nineteenth-century tradition of utilitarianism and secularism which is reducing modern education to a disintegrated mass of specialisms and vocational courses.

It is the function of higher education to rise above this by giving the mind a unifying vision of the spiritual sources from which Western civilization flowed. This is not the responsibility of the Catholic college alone: it is the common concern of all the universities and colleges which are not under the control of the state. But the Catholic college is in a particularly favorable position to realize those aims, since it has a definite and conscious commitment to Christian culture and Christian values.

VIII. EDUCATION AND THE STATE

Anyone who surveys the literature of modern education cannot help feeling discouraged by the thought of the immense amount of time and labor which has been expended with so little apparent fruit. Yet we must not forget that behind this smoke-screen of blue-books and hand-books great forces are at work which have changed the lives and thoughts of men more effectively than the arbitrary power of dictators or the violence of political revolutions.

During the last hundred or two hundred years mankind has been subjected to a process which makes for uniformity and universality. For example, there is universal military service, there is universal suffrage and finally there is universal education. We cannot say that any one of these has caused the others, but they have all influenced one another and they are all presumably the expression of similar or identical forces operating in different fields.

Of these three examples I have given, universal suffrage is usually regarded as the most important. But it is less typical than the others because it is less compulsory. Indeed in the past the use of political suffrage has never been universal, even in societies in which every adult possessed the right to vote. Universal military service, on the other hand, has had less attention paid to it than it deserves. It is the earliest of the three and has its roots deepest in history. It is also the one in which the element of compulsion is strongest and most effective. In England, however, and still more in the United States and the Dominions, its introduction has been so long delayed that it is still regarded as an exceptional emergency measure and has not fully been assimilated by our society and culture.

There remains universal education, which is in fact the most universal of the three, since it has now extended all over the world. Moreover it goes deeper than the other two, since it is directly concerned with the human mind and with the formation of character. It is moreover a continually expanding force, for when once the State has accepted full responsibility for the education of the whole youth of the nation, it is obliged to extend its control further and further into new fields: to the physical welfare of its pupils—to their feeding and medical care—to their amusements and the use of their spare time—and finally to their moral welfare and their psychological guidance.

Thus universal education involves the creation of an immense machinery of organization and control which must go on growing in power and influence until it covers the whole field of culture and embraces every form of educational institution from the nursery school to the university.

Hence the modern movement towards universal education inevitably tends to become the rival or the alternative to the Church, which is also a universal institution and is also concerned directly with the human mind and with the formation of character. And in fact there is no doubt that the progress of universal education has coincided with the secularization of modern culture and has been very largely responsible for it.

In the philosophy of the Enlightenment which inspired the educational policy of the French Revolution and of Continental Liberalism, the Church and the influence of religion were regarded as powers of darkness that were responsible for the backward condition of the masses, and consequently the movement for universal education was a crusade of enlightenment which was inevitably anti-clerical in spirit. Even in England, as recently as 1870, Joseph Chamberlain could declare that "the object of the Liberal party in England, throughout the continent of Europe and in America has been to wrest the education of the young out of the hands of the priests, to whatever denomination they might belong."

In practice no doubt, universal education in England as in Germany and many other countries was the result either of a process of co-operation between Church and State or at least of some kind of *modus vivendi* between them. Nevertheless at best it was an unequal partnership: the fact that secular education is universal and compulsory, while religious education is partial and voluntary, inevitably favors the former and places the Church at a very great disadvantage in educational matters. This is not merely due to the disproportion in wealth and power of a religious minority as compared with the modern state. Even more important is the all-pervading influence of the secular standards and values which affects the whole educational system and makes the idea of an integrated religious culture seem antiquated and absurd to the politicians and the publicists and the technical experts who are the makers of public opinion.

Moreover we must remember that modern secularism, in education as in politics, is not a purely negative force. Today, as in the days of the Enlightenment and the Revolution, it has its ideals and its dogmas—we may almost say that it has its own religion. One of the outstanding exponents of this secular idealism in recent times was the late Professor Dewey, whose ideas have had a profound influence on modern American education, as I described in the last chapter.

Now Dewey, in spite of his secularism, had a conception of education which was almost purely religious. Education is not concerned with intellectual values, its end is not to communicate knowledge or to train scholars in the liberal arts. It exists simply to serve democracy; and democracy is not a form of government, it is a spiritual community, based on "the participation of every human being in the formation of social values." Thus every child is a potential member of the democratic church, and it is the function of education to actualize his membership and to widen his powers of participation. No doubt knowledge is indispensable, but knowledge is always secondary to activity, and activity is secondary to participation. The ultimate end of the whole process is a state of spiritual communion in which every individual shares in the experience of the whole and contributes according to his powers to the formation of "the final pooled intelligence," to use Dewey's expression, which is the democratic mind.

Now it seems to me obvious that this concept of education is a religious one in spite of its secularism. It is inspired by a faith in democracy and a democratic "mystique" which is religious rather than political in spirit. Words like "community," "progress," "life," and "youth," etc., but above all "democracy" itself, have acquired a kind of numinous character which gives them an emotional or evocative power and puts them above rational criticism. But when it comes to the question of the real significance and content of education we cannot help asking what these sacred abstractions really amount to. Do not the most primitive and barbarous peoples known to us achieve these great ends of social participation and communal experience no less completely by their initiation ceremonies and tribal dances than any modern educationalist with his elaborate programs for the integration of the school with life and the sharing of common experience.

The forefather of modern education, who was more consistent than his descendants, Jean Jacques Rousseau, would perhaps have approved of this, since he believed that civilization was on the whole a mistake and that man would be better without it. But the modern democrat usually has rather a naive faith in modern civilization, and he wishes to accept the inheritance of culture, while rejecting the painful process of social and intellectual discipline by which that inheritance has been acquired and transmitted.

In this he differs from the Communist, who shares the same ideal of "participation" and the communalization of experience, but who has a very definite belief in the necessity of authority and social discipline and whose system of education is based not only on a common doctrine but also on a psychological technique for arousing faith and devotion.

The democrat, on the other hand, has no use for authority either in the State or in the school or in the sphere of cultural activity. But when it comes to the question of religious authority, the democrat and the Communist once more find themselves in agreement. As one of Dewey's supporters, Sidney Hook, has pointed out, the philosophy of Dewey, especially in education, is the enemy number one of "every doctrine which holds that man should tend to a supernatural end, in function of which he ought to organize his earthly life."

I have paid so much attention to Dewey's views because of the enormous influence he has had on American education and, through America, on educational ideas in the Far East and elsewhere. Moreover, his views are important because they state in a simplified and explicit form principles that have been taken for granted by liberal or democratic educationalists everywhere. The fact is that modern society was inevitably committed to something of this kind as soon as it abandoned the purely utilitarian conception of education which was characteristic of the English Radical reforms in the early nineteenth century. Henceforward universal education ceased to be considered as a means of communicating learning and became instead an instrument for creating a common mind. In this way universal education becomes the most important agent in the creation of the new secular religion of the state or the national community, which in democratic as well as totalitarian societies is replacing the old religion of the Church as the working religion of the modern world.

I do not, of course, mean to suggest that the democratic ideal is the same as the totalitarian one. For as I have already said with regard to Communism, totalitarian education, like the rest of the totalitarian way of life, is far more authoritarian and is the instrument of an exclusive and intolerant party ideology. The democratic ideal of education is, as Dewey says, an education for freedom—for freedom of thought no less than for freedom of action—and he criticized the traditional forms of education because they retained the authoritarian principle alike in the relation of teacher to pupil and by imposing an absolute standard of culture which the uneducated are forced to accept and admire.

But for this very reason the traditional forms of religious education are the worst of all, because they are the most authoritarian and go furthest in asserting the existence of absolute truths and absolute moral standards to which the individual must conform. In this respect democratic educationalists like Dewey are at one with anti-Catholic propagandists like Mr. Blanshard. To the latter, it is precisely the Catholic attitude to public education which is the basis of his indictment. It is not that he objects to religion as such; for so long as religion is regarded as a private matter which only concerns the conscience and the feelings of the individual, it is a very good thing. But the moment that it attempts to create its own community of thought and to separate its adherents from the common mind of the democratic society and from the State school which is the organ of that common mind, it becomes an anti-social force which every good democrat must reject and condemn.

It is obvious that the whole question of the relations of education to State, Church, community and culture is inextricably involved with fundamental issues which cannot be avoided however we may try to do so. Neither secularism nor Christianity necessarily involves persecution. But both of them can easily become intolerant, and whether they are tolerant or intolerant they are inevitably and in every field irreconcilable with one another. On the one hand we have the secular view that the State is the universal community and the Church is a limited association of groups of individuals for limited ends. On the other there is the Christian view that the Church is the universal community and that the State is a limited association for certain limited ends. The philosopher and the theologian may say that both are perfect societies with their own rights and their proper autonomous spheres of action. But this is only true juridically speaking, not psychologically or morally. The Church is socially incomplete unless there is a Christian society as well as an ecclesiastical congregation, and the State is morally incomplete without some spiritual bond other than the law and the power of the sword. Ever since the loss of a living contact with the historic faith of Christendom modern society has been seeking to find such a bond, either in the democratic ideal of the natural society and its general will, or in the nationalist cult of a historic racial community, or in the Communist faith in the revolutionary mission of the proletariat. And in each case what we find is a substitute religion or counter-religion which transcends the juridical limits of the political State and creates a kind of secular Church.

It is, of course, true that this development has been almost entirely a continental one which finds its characteristic expressions in French revolutionary democracy, German nationalism and Russian communism. England and America, on the other hand, have always followed a different tradition, and their classical political doctrines in the past have been based on the older conception of a limited State which confined itself to certain specific activities and left the larger part of life as an open field for the free activity of individuals and independent organizations. Now in practice this Anglo-Saxon conception of the limited State was closely connected with a sectarian conception of the Church. Religion was active and influential, but it was not united. The dominant issue was not Church and State, but Church and sect, or State, Church and sect, so that in England the formal secularization of the State was not due to an anti-clerical attack on religious belief, but was the work of pious Nonconformists who were concerned above all with the defence of their own religious liberties and privileges.

All this has had an immense influence on the history of English education. For education is one of the forms of activity which traditionally lie outside the competence of a limited State. The fact that public education, as in the universities and the public schools, was Anglican was an inheritance from the Catholic past; and it depended not on education acts and government policy but on the foundation statutes of the educational institutions themselves, which were autonomous corporations, often very jealous of any interference by parliament or governments.

When elementary education was introduced in the nineteenth century it was regarded as the business of the Church of England and of the sects—a kind of extension of the old system of catechism classes and Sunday schools. Even an independent movement like Shaftesbury's Ragged Schools, which was undenominational, was nevertheless essentially religious and antigovernmental in spirit and opposed to any form of State control.

In England, therefore, and also in the United States, the victory of secular education has been due above all to interdenominational friction and jealousy, not to any conscious hostility to religion itself. But at the same time the whole relation of State and community has been changing, owing to the growing responsibility of the State for social and individual welfare and its increasing control of economic life. The continental conception of the State as an all-embracing community, a kind of secular church, has entered as it were by the back door and has gradually and inevitably destroyed the traditional conception of the limited State and drastically reduced the sphere of action of non-political organizations in education and social life generally. In some respects we are now worse off than the continental peoples, since there is no place in our traditions for the idea of a concordat as a kind of treaty between Church and State considered as two autonomous societies.

In the United States above all, the principle of the absolute separation of Church and State has been carried so far that it involves a refusal to recognize the Church as a corporate entity, so that anything of the nature of a concordat would be regarded as a violation of the Constitution. Similarly in the domain of public education, the principle of the separation of Church and State is now interpreted so rigorously as to ban any kind of positive Christian teaching from the school, with the result that the educational system inevitably favors the pagan and secularist minority against the Christian and Jewish elements who probably represent a large majority of the population.

Now this leads, on the one hand, to the propagation of that kind of substitute religion which I have already described as the established faith of the democratic state; and on the other hand, to the devaluation of traditional religion as unessential, non-vital, exceptional and perhaps even unsocial.

No doubt there are some American Protestants who are so convinced of the moral values of the democratic way of life that they tend to identify the democratic substitute religion with their own rather indefinite Christian tradition. One such Protestant educationalist asserts that—"to call public education 'godless' betrays invincible ignorance, infinite prejudice and complete misunderstanding of what religion is about," since "the public school is more distinctly a faith of all the people than the Church"[1] itself.

I do not suppose that such utterances are representative of orthodox Protestant opinion. Certainly they would be rejected by every Catholic. Yet even Catholics are not immune from the pervasive influence of secularism in education. But this influence shows itself in two opposite ways. In so far as Catholics preserve their own schools and universities by great efforts and sacrifices,

[1] C. H. Moehlman, *School and Church: The American Way* (New York, Harper, 1944).

they are forced to devote so much energy to the mere material or technical work of keeping the system going, that the quality of their teaching suffers. They become more concerned with the utilitarian need for practical results, as measured by the competitive standards set by the State or the secular educational system, than with the essential problem of the transmission of Catholic culture. And in the second place the strength and pervasiveness of secular culture forces Christians, Catholic as well as Protestant, to accept the sectarian solution, which acquiesces in the secularization of culture and social life and strives in compensation to maintain a strict standard of religious observance inside the closed doors of the conventicle and the home.

The most remarkable example of this system, applied with rigid consistency over a period of many centuries, is to be seen in the life of the Jewish community in the ghettos of Central and Eastern Europe. But the ghetto was, after all, a solution imposed from without, and it would never have existed without a certain amount of active persecution and a very strong element of racial prejudice and national self-consciousness. Where these factors exist among Christians, as for example in the case of the Irish mass immigration into Great Britain and the United States in the middle of the nineteenth century, we do get something like the formation of a Christian ghetto where a minority inspired by an intense religious patriotism lives its own spiritual life under the surface of a dominant hostile culture.

But there is no longer any room for a ghetto in the modern secular state. Both its tolerance and its intolerance are hostile to the existence of any such closed world. Under modern conditions the sectarian solution merely means that the religious minority abdicates its claim to influence the culture of the community. And the attempt to use religious education in order to enforce a rigid standard of religious practice in the midst of a secular culture only results in increasing the problem of "leakage." And thus we get a situation in which the Catholics who both practise and understand their religion are the minority of a minority, and the majority of the population are neither fully Christian nor consciously atheist, but non-practising Catholics, half-Christians and well-meaning people who are devoid of any positive religious knowledge at all.

Hence it is not enough for Catholics to confine their efforts to the education of the Catholic minority. If they want to preserve Catholic education in a secularized society, they have got to do something about non-Catholic education also. The future of civilization depends on the fate of the majority, and so long as nothing is done to counteract the present trend of modern education the mind of the masses must become increasingly alienated from the whole tradition of Christian culture.

But this is not inevitable. It need never have happened if Christians had not been so absorbed in their internal conflicts that they adopted a negative defensive attitude towards the problem of national education as a whole. In England, at any rate, there has never been a time when public policy in education has been actively or consciously anti-Christian. Indeed some of the leading representatives of the Board of Education, like Matthew Arnold, were more fully aware of the dangers of secularization and the cultural importance of religious education than were the religious leaders themselves.

The situation has, of course, deteriorated considerably since Arnold's day, especially in the higher studies. Theology, which once dominated the university, has now been pushed from the center to the circumference and has become a specialism among an increasing number of specialisms, while the study of divinity as an integral part of the general curriculum of studies, which still survived in a vestigial form before World War I, has disappeared entirely. I do not suggest that it is possible, or perhaps even desirable, to restore it. What I do believe very strongly is that the time has come to consider the possibility of introducing the study of Christian culture as an objective historical reality into the curriculum of university studies.

Until a man acquires some knowledge of another culture, he cannot be said to be educated, since his whole outlook is so conditioned by his own social environment that he does not realize its limitations. He is a provincial in time, if not in place, and he almost inevitably tends to accept the standards and values of his own society as absolute. The widening of the intellectual horizon by initiation into a different world of culture was indeed the most valuable part of the old classical education.

The study of Christian culture would, I believe, provide a really effective substitute. It would initiate the student into a world that was unknown or at best half known, and at the same time it would deepen his knowledge of modern culture by showing its genetic relation to the culture of the past. No one denies the existence of a Christian literature, a Christian philosophy and a Christian institutional order, but at present these are never studied as parts of an organic whole. Yet without this integrated study it is impossible to understand even the development of the modern vernacular literature.

But how does this affect the question of Christian education? Obviously the academic study of Christian culture as an historical phenomenon is no substitute for religious education in the ordinary sense. What it might do, however, is to help to remove the preliminary prejudice against the Christian view of things which plays so large a part in the secularization of culture. The fact is that the average educated person is not only ignorant of Christian theology, he is no less ignorant of Christian philosophy, Christian history and Christian literature, and in short of Christian culture in general. And he is not ashamed of his ignorance, because Christianity has come to be one of the things that educated people don't talk about. This is quite a recent prejudice which arose among the half-educated and gradually spread upwards and downwards. It did not exist among civilized people in the nineteenth century, whatever their personal beliefs were. Men like Lord Melbourne and Macaulay could talk as intelligently about religious subjects as Gladstone and Acton. It was only at the very end of the century that Christianity ceased to be intellectually respectable and it was due not only to the secularization of culture but also to the general lowering of cultural standards that characterized the age.

Today there are signs of an improvement in this respect. Religion has come back into poetry and fiction, and there is once more a civilized interest in religious discussion. But this cannot go far unless religion is brought back into higher education, and this can only be achieved by giving the systematic study of Christian culture a recognized place in university studies.

A reform of this kind on the level of higher studies would inevitably penetrate the lower levels of secondary and primary teaching and by degrees affect the whole tone of public education. It is obviously difficult to improve the situation in the schools if the teachers have no knowledge of Christian culture and if the standard set by the university is a secular one. However, it is for the universities and the other centers of higher education to take the first step; and if they did so, there is little doubt that they would find plenty of support elsewhere, and that their initiation of the study of Christian culture would be most fruitful in results.

PART TWO

THE SITUATION OF CHRISTIAN EDUCATION IN THE MODERN WORLD

IX. THE STUDY OF WESTERN CULTURE

One of the chief defects of modern education has been its failure to find an adequate method for the study of our own civilization. The old humanist education taught all that it knew about the civilization of ancient Greece and Rome, and taught little else. In the nineteenth century, this aristocratic and humanist ideal was gradually replaced by the democratic utilitarianism of compulsory state education, on the one hand, and by the ideal of scientific specialization, on the other.

The result has been an intellectual anarchy imperfectly controlled by the crude methods of the examination system and of payment by results. The mind of the student is overwhelmed and dazed by the volume of new knowledge which is being accumulated by the labor of specialists, while the necessity for using education as a stepping-stone to a profitable career leaves him little time to stop and think. And the same is true of the teacher, who has become a kind of civil servant tied to a routine over which he can have little control.

Now the old humanist education, with all its limitations and faults, possessed something that modern education has lost. It possessed an intelligible form, owing to the fact that the classical culture which it studied was seen as a whole, not only in its literary manifestations but also in its social structure and its historical development. Modern education has lacked this formal unity, because it has never attempted to study modern civilization with the care and earnestness which humanist education devoted to classical culture. Consequently, the common background of humanist culture has been lost, and modern education finds its goal in competing specialisms.

It is in America that this centrifugal tendency in modern education has found its extreme development, and it is here that attempts are now being made to find a cure for the disease. Typical examples of this movement are to be seen in the Columbia Introduction to the Study of Western Civilization, the similar course at Princeton and the Annapolis Great Books programme. We may also mention the proposals of Dr. A. E. Bestor for the study of American civilization as a foundation for liberal education, which are contained in the final chapter of his book *Educational Wastelands* (1953). All the programmes are concerned in one way or other with the study of Western culture as an intelligible unity. They accept the existing situation of vocational studies and multiple specializations, and they attempt to correct these centrifugal tendencies by giving students a common cultural background and the consciousness of the existence of a world of thought and cultural activity which includes and transcends every specialized study.

Though the courses are devoted to Western civilization as a whole, by far the greater part of the modern material used is provided by five countries—England, the United States, France, Germany and Italy. Nevertheless, though a change of distribution would have done more justice to the contribution of the smaller nations to European culture, it would have made very little difference to the general character of the whole. For the main strands of Western civilization are so closely interwoven that all of them are represented in each of its several parts.

This organic unity of Western culture is so strong that even the modern developments of extreme nationalism have been incapable of creating any real cultural and spiritual autarky. Indeed, if they go beyond a certain point in this direction they prove fatal to the existence of the national culture itself, as the catastrophic development of national socialism in Germany has shown. Every great movement in the history of Western civilization from the Carolingian age to the nineteenth century has been an international movement which owed its existence and its development to the co-operation of many different peoples.

The unitary national state which has played so great a part in modern history is no doubt a characteristically European institution. Yet it represents only one aspect of Western civilization. On the other side there is the still older tradition of co-operation between cities and institutions and individuals. This existed before the unitary state was ever thought of, and still survives in so far as the tradition of European religion and science still preserves its vitality. The intercourse between the Mediterranean and the North or between the Atlantic and Central Europe was never purely economic or political; it also meant the exchange of knowledge and ideas and the influence of social institutions and artistic and literary forms. The conception of a community of Western culture is no new idea. It has always been accepted in one form or another as a fact of daily experience and as an axiom of historical thought.

No doubt there have been great differences of opinion as to the nature of this community; nor is this surprising since, whatever its nature, the unity of Western civilization is certainly not a simple thing. In contrast to the monolithic simplicity of the great oriental cultures, the civilization of the West is like a Gothic cathedral, a complex mechanism of conflicting pressures which achieves its unity by the dynamic balance of thrust and counterthrust.

The two great traditions that have contributed most to the development of Western civilization—the inheritance of classical culture and the Christian religion—have always produced an internal tension in the spirit of our culture which shows itself in the conflict between the extreme ideals of other-worldly asceticism and secular humanism. Yet the coexistence of both of these elements has been an essential condition of the Western development, one which has inspired all the great achievements of our culture. But there is also a third element, which was ignored or taken for granted in the past and which has only attained full consciousness and intellectual expression during the last two centuries.

This third element is the autochthonous tradition of the Western peoples themselves, as distinct from what they have received from their teachers and school-masters: the original endowment of Western man, which he derives from a remote prehistoric past, which is rooted in the soil of Europe and which finds expression in his languages if not in his literature. This is the factor which has been stressed, often in very one-sided and exaggerated forms, by the modern cult of nationalism, a movement which has resurrected forgotten languages and re-created submerged peoples. It has not only changed the map of Europe, but has had a revolutionary effect on European education and on European literature.

Even if we regard modern nationalism as subversive of the unity of Western culture, even if we accept the saying of the great Austrian poet that "the path of modern culture leads from humanity through nationality to bestiality," we must still admit its importance as a characteristic product of the Western development and a vital factor in modern history. Nor is its importance confined to Europe, since it has proved capable of adaptation and transmission to non-European peoples and has become a world-wide movement which threatens to destroy the hegemony of Western civilization.

It was the creed of the Enlightenment that Western civilization was destined to expand by the progressive influence of science and trade and humanitarian ideals until it became a true world civilization, so that in the distant future our descendants might hope to see "the Parliament of Man, the Federation of the World." This is no ignoble ideal, and it still commands the allegiance of the enlightened elements in Western democracy. But though we have achieved the Parliament of Man and the Federation of the World in the form of the United Nations, we have not got a world civilization; and the very existence of Western civilization itself is in question.

The sublimated idealism of the Enlightenment, the spirit of the League of Nations and of the United Nations Charter have not proved strong enough to control the aggressive dynamism of nationalism. The new type of politics, as we saw it in Fascism and as we see it today in Communism, is a technique of organized violence which may be directed by a cool and realistic will to power, but which owes its driving power to the blind, subconscious forces of racial aggressiveness and social resentment.

No doubt Western civilization has in the past been full of wars and revolutions, and the national elements in our culture, even when they were ignored, always provided an unconscious driving force of passion and aggressive self-assertion. But these elements were kept in check in the past by common spiritual loyalties and by the discipline of an objective intellectual tradition. In fact, the history of Western culture has been the story of the progressive "civilization" of the barbaric energy of Western man and the progressive subordination of nature to human purpose under the twofold influence of Christian ethics and scientific reason. Above all, no other culture in the world has devoted so much attention to the problem of political power and the moral principles of political action as that of the West. It has been debated down the centuries by Dante and St. Thomas, by Machiavelli and Bodin, Hobbes and Harrington, Locke and Burke, Montesquieu and Rousseau, Hegel and Mill, de Maistre and Proudhon.

This freedom of political discussion on the highest level is something which Western civilization has in common with that of classical antiquity, but with no other. It presupposes the existence of an international body of educated opinion which is not the creature of the state and which is free to discuss ultimate social and political principles in an atmosphere of relative impartiality. But modern nationalism leaves no room for scientific impartiality. It takes all it can from the common treasure of European culture and rejects with hostility and contempt all that it cannot claim as its own. It divides the republic of letters by a civil war of rival propaganda which is as ruthless and unscrupulous as civil wars have always been. At the same time, the state has armed itself with the new weapons of psychological warfare, mass suggestion and disintegration which threaten mankind with a spiritual tyranny more formidable than anything that the world has hitherto known.

These tendencies are equally fatal to the unity of Western civilization and to the creation of an international world order such as has been envisaged by the Charters of the League of

Nations and the United Nations. The conflict is therefore not one between Europe and the other world cultures. It is a malady that is common to modern civilization in all its forms and in every continent. But there is no doubt that the crisis appears in its most acute form in Europe, where more than twenty national states, including some of the most highly developed military and industrial powers in the world, are crowded together in a smaller area than that of the United States. Under these conditions, every European war has the characteristics of a civil war, and the creation of an international order is no longer the dream of political idealists but has become a practical necessity without which Europe cannot hope to survive.

The great question of the present century is whether Western civilization is strong enough to create a world order based on the principles of international law and personal liberty that are the fruits of the whole tradition of Western political thought, or whether we are witnessing the emergence of a series of gigantic continental mass states which will organize the world into a small number of exclusive and antagonistic spheres of power.

At the present moment the prospects of the realization of the second alternative seem threatening enough, and Europe has been so disintegrated by war and political conflicts that it has lost its old position of cultural leadership. Nevertheless, it would be unsafe to judge the situation on the present balance of material resources. The forces of Western civilization are greater than the economic and military resources of the states of Western Europe. One of the greatest of the non-European world powers, the United States, is so profoundly impregnated with Western traditions and ideals that America cannot accept the complete disintegration of Europe without imperiling her own cultural existence.

Whatever may be the political future of Europe and however dark are her economic prospects, Europe retains her historic position as the source of Western civilization, and this is bound to influence the future as well as the past. For it is hardly too much to say that modern civilization *is* Western civilization. There are very few forces living and moving in the modern world which have not been either developed or transformed by the influence of Western culture.

It is therefore as important as it ever was to understand the nature of Western civilization and how it was that this relatively minute group of European states came to transform the rest of the world and to change the whole course of human history. Hence a systematic study of Western civilization has become a necessary part of education, not only in Europe itself, but still more in the non-European lands which still belong to the tradition of Western civilization. It is necessary too, in the Oriental societies which are ceasing to be politically and economically dependent on Western imperialism but which still have to find a synthesis between their traditional cultures and the new ideas and the new ways of life which they have derived from the West.

Even if the Western attempts to create an international world order as a safeguard of peace and freedom prove an illusion and the world descends into a twilight of barbarism and a new dark age begins, this task at least remains.

For even the Dark Ages that followed the fall of the Roman Empire did not entirely destroy the continuity of culture, owing to the fact that an elementary knowledge of classical civilization was preserved and transmitted by the monks and schoolmen

who were the educators of the Christian barbarians. No doubt
the culture of the ancient world was more easily transmissible
than our own because it was infinitely simpler and because it had
behind it the strong unitary traditions of the Roman Empire and
the Christian Church. Nevertheless even our own complex and
many-sided civilization is not entirely formless. It has an intellectual tradition which is capable of being formulated and transmitted no less than that of classical culture. How this can best be
done is the greatest problem of modern education, and we are
still far from finding a solution. In some respects it may prove
easier to approach the problem in America than in Europe, not
only because the New World is able to see the European
achievement in perspective, but also because from the American
standpoint there is a clear intelligible relation between the history of the United States and that of Europe as a whole. In
Europe itself this is not the case. The student starts with one
particular national tradition, and he becomes involved in a study
of the intricate pattern of conflicting national traditions before
he has become fully aware of the existence or the nature of
European civilization as an organic whole.

In the United States, however, there is a general agreement
today that nationality provides too narrow a basis for historical
study and there is consequently a general move towards some
wider alternative. But what are the alternatives? World history
or the study of civilization in general is too vast a study to be
covered, even superficially, in a two- or three-year course. If
we follow Dr. Toynbee's concept of the true unit of history
being the civilization, then Western civilization is the obvious
subject for study. But, as Dr. Toynbee himself has shown,
Western civilization is inseparable from Christian civilization,
and the latter is the more fundamental and intelligible unit. By

studying Christian culture in its several forms we are led to understand Western civilization from within outwards; whereas it is much more difficult to achieve a unitary study if we begin with the centrifugal multiplicity of Western civilization and attempt to discover its principle of unity by going from without inwards. But if we begin our study with Christian culture we immediately discover the sources of the moral values of Western culture, as well as the sources of the intellectual traditions that have determined the course of Western education.

For, as I have written elsewhere:

The activity of the Western mind, which manifested itself alike in scientific and technical invention as well as in geographical discovery, was not the natural inheritance of a particular biological type; it was the result of a long process of education which gradually changed the orientation of human thought and enlarged the possibilities of social action. In this process the vital factor was not the aggressive power of conquerors and capitalists, but the widening of the capacity of human intelligence and the development of new types of creative genius and ability.[1]

[1] *Religion and the Rise of Western Culture* (1950), p. 10.

X. THE CASE FOR THE STUDY
OF CHRISTIAN CULTURE

At first sight it may seem surprising that there is any need for
the discussion of Christian culture study, at least among Catholic
educationalists, for one would have expected that the whole
question would have been thrashed out years ago and there was
no longer room for any difference of opinion. But as a matter of
fact this is far from being the case, and the more one looks into
the subject, the more one is struck by the vagueness and un-
certainty of educated opinion in this matter and the lack of any
accepted doctrine or educational policy.

No doubt the situation in all the English-speaking countries
differs essentially from that of Catholic Europe, where the
Church has either preserved a privileged position in educational
matters or, more frequently, has been forced to resist the hostile
pressure of an anti-clerical or "laicist" regime. The Catholics of
the English-speaking countries, in England as well as in America
and in Australia, have not had the need to face the continental
type of political anti-clericalism, but on the other hand, they
have no privileged position and no publicly established educational institutions of their own. They have had to build their
whole educational system from the bottom upwards with their
own scanty resources. And so the main problem of Catholic
education in the English-speaking countries has been the prob-

lem of the primary school—how to secure the necessary minimum of religious instruction for their children.

The urgency of this issue has relegated all the problems of higher education to the second place. Catholics have felt that if they can save the schools, the universities can look after themselves. And in fact they have done so, up to a point. Catholics have managed to adapt themselves fairly successfully to the English and American systems of higher education. Nevertheless it has been a question of adaptation to an external system, and there has been little opportunity to decide what the nature of higher education should be or to create their own curriculum of studies.

All this is comparatively simple. But it is much more difficult to explain the situation in the past, when the Church dominated the whole educational system—schools, colleges and universities —and determined the whole course of higher studies. Surely one would have expected that the study of Christian culture would have formed the basis for the higher studies and that the foundations of an educational tradition would have been laid which would have dominated Christian education ever since. But what actually happened was that for centuries higher education has been so identified with the study of one particular historic culture—that of ancient Greece and Rome—that there was no room left for anything else. Even the study of our own particular national culture, including both history and literature, did not obtain full recognition until the nineteenth century, while the concept of Christian culture as an object of study has never been recognized at all.

The great obstacle to this study has not been religious or secularist prejudices but strictly cultural. It had its origins in the idealization of classical antiquity by the humanist scholars and artists of the fifteenth and sixteenth centuries. And it followed from this conception that the period that intervened between the fall of Rome and the Renaissance offered the historian, as Voltaire says, "the barren prospect of a thousand years of stupidity and barbarism." They were "middle ages" in the original sense of the word—that is, a kind of cultural vacuum between two ages of cultural achievement which (to continue the same quotation) "vindicate the greatness of the human spirit."

This view, which necessarily ignores the achievements and even the existence of Christian culture, was passed on almost unchanged from the Renaissance to the eighteenth-century Enlightenment and from the latter to the modern secularist ideologies. And though today every instructed person recognizes that it is based on a completely erroneous view of history and very largely on a sheer ignorance of history, it still continues to exert an immense influence, both consciously and unconsciously, on modern education and on our attitude to the past.

It is therefore necessary for educators to make a positive effort to exorcise the ghost of this ancient error and to give the study of Christian culture the place it deserves in modern education. We cannot leave this to the medievalists alone, for they are to some extent themselves tied to the error by the limitations of their specialism. Christian culture is not the same thing as medieval culture. It existed before the Middle Ages began and it continued to exist after they had ended. We cannot understand medieval culture unless we study its foundations in the age of the Fathers and the Christian Empire, and we cannot understand the classical vernacular literatures of post-Renaissance Europe unless we study their roots in medieval culture. Even the Renaissance itself, as Conrad Burdach and E. R. Curtius have shown, is not intelligible unless it is studied as part of a movement which had its origins deep in the Middle Ages.

Moreover, it seems that the time is ripe for a new approach to the subject, since our educational system—and not in one country alone, but throughout the Western world—is passing through a period of rapid and fundamental change. The old domination of classical humanism has passed away, and nothing has taken its place except the scientific specialisms which do not provide a complete intellectual education, and rather tend to disintegrate into technologies. Every educator recognizes that this is unsatisfactory. A scientific specialist or a technologist is not an educated person. He tends to become merely an instrument of the industrialist or the bureaucrat, a worker ant in an insect society, and the same is true of the literary specialist, though his social function is less obvious.

But even the totalitarians do not accept this solution; on the contrary, they insist most strongly on the importance of the cultural element in education whether their ideal of culture is nationalist and racial, as with the Nazis, or cosmopolitan and proletarian, as with the Communists. No doubt from our point of view this totalitarian culture means the forcible indoctrination of scientist and worker alike with the same narrow party ideology, but at least it does provide a simple remedy for the disintegrating effects of modern specialization and gives the whole educational system a unifying purpose.

Heaven forbid that we should try to solve our educational problems in this way by imposing a compulsory political ideology on the teacher and the scientist! But we cannot avoid this evil by sitting back and allowing higher education to degenerate into a chaos of competing specialisms without any guidance for the student except the urgent practical necessity of finding a job and making a living as soon as his education is finished. This combination of utilitarianism and specialism is not only fatal to the idea of a liberal education, it is also one of the main causes of the intellectual disintegration of modern Western culture under the aggressive threat of totalitarian nationalism and Communism.

Some cultural education is necessary if Western culture is to survive, but we can no longer rely exclusively on the traditional discipline of classical humanism, though this is the source of all that was best in the tradition of Western liberalism and Western science. For we cannot ignore the realities of the situation—the progressive decline of the great tradition of Western humanism, the dwindling number of classical scholars and the development of a vast nation-wide system of professional education which has nothing in common with the old classical culture.

Nevertheless the decline of classical studies does not necessarily involve the decline of liberal education itself. In America the liberal arts college still maintains its prestige and American educationalists have continued to advocate the ideals of liberal education. But there is still no general agreement on how the lost unity of humanist education can be recovered. The liberal arts college itself tends to disintegrate under the growing number of subjects until it becomes an amorphous collection of alternative courses. It is to remedy this state of things that American educationalists have introduced or proposed a general integrative study of our culture which would provide a common intellectual background for the students of the liberal arts.

The problem for Catholics is a somewhat different one. They have never altogether lost sight of the medieval ideal of an order and hierarchy of knowledge and the integration of studies from above by a higher spiritual principle. In other words Catholics have a common theology and a common philosophy—the unitive disciplines which the modern secular system of higher education lacks. Yet in spite of this enormous advantage it cannot be claimed that the Catholic university has solved the problem of modern higher education or that it stands out as a brilliant exception from the educational chaos of the rest of the world. For the Catholic liberal arts college suffers from very much the same weaknesses as the secular ones. It is losing ground externally in relation to the other schools within the university, and internally it is becoming disintegrated by the multiplicities of different studies and courses. And the reason for this is that Catholic education has suffered no less—perhaps even more—than secular education from the decline of classical studies and the loss of the old humanist culture. This was the keystone of the whole educational structure, and when it was removed the higher studies of theology and philosophy became separated from the world of specialist and vocational studies which inevitably absorb the greater part of the time and money and personnel of the modern university.

It is therefore of vital importance to maintain the key position of the liberal arts college in the university and to save the liberal arts course from further disintegration. And it is with these ends in view that I have made my suggestions for the study of Christian culture as a means of integration and unity. Its function would be very similar to that of the general courses in contemporary civilization, Western civilization, or American culture which are actually in operation in some of the non-Catholic universities. Indeed it is the same thing adapted to the needs of Catholic higher studies. For if we study Western culture in the light of Catholic theology and philosophy, we are in fact studying Christian culture or one aspect of it. I believe that the study of Christian culture is the missing link which it is essential to supply if the tradition of Western education and Western culture is to survive, for it is only through this study that we can understand how Western culture came to exist and what are the essential values for which it stands.

I see no reason to suppose, as some have argued, that such a study would have a narrowing and cramping effect on the mind of the student. On the contrary, it is eminently a liberal and liberalizing study, since it shows us how to relate our own contemporary social experience to the wider perspectives of universal history. For, after all, Christian culture is nothing to be ashamed of. It is no narrow sectarian tradition. It is one of the four great historic civilizations on which the modern world is founded. If modern education fails to communicate some understanding of this great tradition, it has failed in one of its most essential tasks. For the educated person cannot play his full part in modern life unless he has a clear sense of the nature and achievements of Christian culture: how Western civilization became Christian and how far it is Christian today and in what ways it has ceased to be Christian: in short, a knowledge of our Christian roots and of the abiding Christian elements in Western culture.

When I speak of Western culture I am not using the word in the limited sense in which it was used by Matthew Arnold and the humanists, who were concerned only with the highest level of cultivated intelligence, but in the sense of the anthropologists and social historians, who have widened it out to cover the whole pattern of human life and thought in a living society. In this sense of the word, a culture is a definite historical unity, but as Dr. Toynbee explains so clearly in the Introduction to his *Study of History*, it has a much wider expansion in space and time than any purely political unit, and it alone constitutes an intelligible field of historical study, since no part of it can be properly understood except in relation to the whole.

Behind the existing unity of Western culture we have the older unity of Christian culture which is the historic basis of our civilization. For more than a thousand years from the conversion of the Roman Empire down to the Reformation the peoples of Europe were fully conscious of their membership in the great Christian society and accepted the Christian faith and the Christian moral law as the ultimate bond of social unity and the spiritual basis of their way of life. Even after the unity of Christendom had been broken by the Reformation, the tradition of Christian culture still survived in the culture and institutions of the different European peoples, and in some cases exists even in the midst of our secularized culture, as we see so strikingly in the English monarch's coronation rite.

Consequently anyone who wishes to understand our own culture as it exists today cannot dispense with the study of Christian culture, whether he is a Christian or not. Indeed in some ways this study is more necessary for the secularist than for the Christian, because he lacks that ideological key to the understanding of the past which every Christian ought to possess.

The subject is a vast one which could occupy the lifetime of an advanced scholar. But the same may be said of the study of Western civilization in the secular universities, or indeed of the study of classical culture in the past. Nevertheless it can also provide the ordinary student who is going out into the world to earn his living in professional life with a glimpse of the intellectual and spiritual riches to which he is heir and to which he can return in later years for light and refreshment.

If the college or university can only inspire its students with a sense of the value of this inheritance and a desire to know more about it, it will have taken the first and most essential step. No doubt higher education is not unaware of this need and has made some attempt to satisfy it both in the liberal arts college and in the graduate school. But it has done so hitherto in a somewhat haphazard and piecemeal fashion. The student can study any number of subjects which have a bearing on the subject of Christian culture or form part of it; but none of these will give him any comprehensive view of the whole. What is needed, so it seems to me, is a study of Christian culture as a social reality—its origins, development and achievements—for this would provide a background of framework that would integrate the liberal studies which at present are apt to disintegrate into unrelated specialisms.

This kind of program is not simply a study of the Christian classics; nor is it primarily a literary study. It is a cultural study in the sociological and historical sense, and it would devote more attention to the social institutions and the moral values of Christian culture than to its literary and artistic achievements. Christian culture has indeed flowered again and again in literature and art, and these successive flowerings are well worthy of our study. But obviously it is out of the question to make the average arts student study all of them. Such a proposal, which one critic of Christian culture study assumes to be my intention, is to misunderstand the nature of the problem. What we need is not an encyclopaedic knowledge of all the products of Christian culture, but a study of the culture-process itself from its spiritual and theological roots, through its organic historical growth to its cultural fruits. It is this organic relation between theology, history and culture which provides the integrative principle in

Catholic higher education, and the only one that is capable of taking the place of the old classical humanism which is disappearing or has already disappeared.

Moreover, if we desire to promote religious and intellectual understanding among the different religious groups within American society, surely the best way to do this is to understand and appreciate our own culture in all its depth and breadth. Without this full cultural awareness it is impossible either to interpret one's culture to others or to understand the problems of intercultural relations, problems which are of such incalculable importance for the future of the modern world.

I do not deny that there are great practical obstacles in the way of this study. The secularist is naturally afraid that it might be used as an instrument of religious propaganda, and he is consequently anxious to minimize the importance of the Christian element in our culture and exaggerate the gulf between modern civilization and the Christian culture of the past.

The Christian, on the other hand, is often afraid lest the historical study of Christian culture should lead to an identification of Christianity with a culture and a social system which belong to the dead past. But for the Christian the past can never be dead, as it often seems to the secularist, since we believe the past and the present are united in the one Body of the Church and that the Christians of the past are still present as witnesses and helpers in the life of the Church today.

No doubt it would be an error to apply this principle to the particular forms of Christian culture which are conditioned by material factors and limited by the change of historical circumstances. But as there is an organic relation between the Christian faith and the Christian life, so also there is a relation between Christian life and Christian culture. The relation between faith and life is completely realized only in the life of the saint. But there has never been a temporal society of saints, and the attempt to create one, as in Puritan England or Massachusetts, represents a sectarian perversion of Christian culture. Nevertheless it is the very nature of the Christian faith and the Christian life to penetrate and change the social environment in which they exist, and there is no aspect of human life which is closed to this leavening and transforming process. Thus Christian culture is the periphery of the circle which has its center in the Incarnation and the faith of the Church and the lives of the saints.

All this is to be seen in history. Christianity did actually come into the historical world and did actually transform the societies with which it came into contact: first, the Hellenistic-Oriental society of the Eastern Roman Empire, and secondly, the Latin and barbarian societies of Western Europe. From this two new cultures were born—the Byzantine culture of the East and Western Christendom, both of which, in spite of their ultimate separation, share a large number of common characteristics.

Both of these cultures have now been secularized, but the process of secularization is so recent and even incomplete that it is absolutely impossible to understand them in their secularized form unless we have studied their Christian past.

Unfortunately it is nobody's business to study or to teach this subject, and it is extremely difficult under existing conditions for anyone to acquire the necessary knowledge, even if he can spare the time and energy to do so. Nevertheless the very reasons which make the study of the subject so difficult are also reasons in its favor from the educational point of view. They are due to the fact that it is an integrative subject involving the cooperation of a number of different specialized studies, in the same way as the study of *litterae humaniores* in the Greats

School at Oxford involves the co-operation of philosophers and historians as well as philologists and literary critics. A curriculum in Christian culture would thus embrace a co-operative study of Christian philosophy, Christian literature and Christian history.

What are the principles upon which such a study should be based? We must recognize that Christian culture can be studied in two ways: externally, as an objective historical study of Christendom as one of the four great world civilizations on which the modern world is founded; and from within, as the study of the history of the Christian people—a study of the ways in which Christianity has expressed itself in human thought and life and institutions through the ages.

The first is necessary for every historian, since it is an essential aspect of the study of world civilization. The second is necessary to the Christian, since it deals with his own spiritual history and with the successive stages of Christian life and thought.

For educational purposes, both these studies should be combined. The student should be given a general knowledge of the external development of Christian civilization from the beginning to the present day, and this should be accompanied by a more detailed study of Christian life and thought and institutions during some one particular period.

The development of Christian culture has passed through six successive phases or periods, each with its distinctive form of culture:

1. Primitive Christianity, from the first to the beginning of the fourth century. This is the age which saw the birth of the Church: the subterranean expansion of the Christian way of life beneath the surface of a pagan civilization and the development of an autonomous Christian society widely distributed

through the great cities of the Roman Empire, above all in the Eastern Mediterranean.

2. Patristic Christianity, from the fourth to the sixth centuries: the age of the conversion of the Roman-Hellenistic world and the establishment of Christian-Roman or Byzantine culture.

3. The Formation of Western Christendom, from the sixth to the eleventh centuries: the age of the conversion of Northern Europe and the formation of Western Christendom through the gradual permeation of the barbarian cultures—Celtic, Germanic, and Slavonic—by Christian influence. At the same time a large part of the old Christian world was lost by the rise of Islam and the development of a new non-Christian culture there.

4. Medieval Christendom, from the eleventh to the fifteenth centuries. This is the age in which Western Christian culture attained full development and cultural consciousness and created new social institutions and new forms of artistic and literary expression.

5. Divided Christendom, from the sixteenth to the eighteenth centuries: the age of the development of the national European cultures. In spite of the internal religious strife which characterized the period, it was also an age of expansion, so that Christian culture gradually came to incorporate the whole of the New World. It also saw a great, though unsuccessful, effort to spread Christianity from Europe to India, China and Japan.

6. Secularized Christendom, from the eighteenth century to the present. During this period Western culture achieved a position of world hegemony, but at the same time it ceased to be Christian, and the old institutional framework of Christian culture was swept away by revolutionary movements. Nevertheless Christianity survived and Western culture still retains

considerable traces of its Christian origins. Moreover the world expansion of Western culture has been accompanied by a new expansion of Christian missionary influence, especially in Africa and Australia.

Each of these periods has its own specific character, which can be studied in art and philosophy, in literature and in social institutions. Most important and characteristic of all are the successive forms of the religious life itself which have manifested themselves in each of the different periods.

This study covers much the same ground chronologically as the general courses in the history of Western civilization, but it has an internal principle of organic unity which they do not possess, and every period and every aspect of a particular period has an organic relation to the whole. It is especially valuable as a co-ordinating study which will help us to understand the resemblances and differences of the different national and regional cultures by explaining the common factors that have influenced them all. Institutions that are common to the whole of Christendom such as monasticism and the university, or even constitutional monarchy and the representative system of government, are none of them entirely explicable within the framework of national history, within which they are usually studied. They can only be understood as parts of a common international heritage of Christian culture. In the same way the spiritual archetypes which formed the character and inspired the life of Western man are of Christian origin, and however imperfectly they were realized in practice, it is impossible to understand his pattern of behavior unless we take account of them.

We study political ideas in relation to history, although we know that the majority of men are never governed by purely ideological motives. How much more then should we study the religious element in culture, for this affected the majority of men from the cradle to the grave and has been a continuous influence on western culture for more than twelve centuries. It was not studied in the past, because men took it for granted like the air they breathed. But now that our civilization is becoming predominantly and increasingly secular, it is necessary to make an express study of it, if we are to understand our past and the nature of the culture that we have inherited.

XI. THE STUDY OF CHRISTIAN CULTURE IN THE CATHOLIC COLLEGE

The study of Christian culture as described in Chapter X offers a new approach to the three great problems that confront Western education at the present time: first, how to maintain the tradition of liberal education against the growing pressure of scientific specialization and utilitarian vocationalism; secondly, how to retain the unity of Western culture against the dissolvent forces of nationalism and racialism; and thirdly, how to preserve the tradition of Christian culture in the age of secularism.

The first two problems concern any Western university or institution for higher education, but the third is the special concern of Catholic colleges and universities since it is the end for which they were created. For them the problem is not simply cultural but religious, since the secularization of education threatens the very existence of the Christian way of life and the Christian community. The traditional system of Catholic education has come down from the days when whatever primary education there was, was religious, so that everyone had a common background of religious instruction. But today the existence of a universal state-provided system of secular education makes it necessary for us to build a whole background of culture and wide general knowledge if our people are not to be swamped by the tide of circumambient materialism.

For modern culture is not pluralistic in character, as some social scientists have assumed; on the contrary, it is more unitary, more uniform and more highly centralized and organized than any culture that the world has known hitherto. And modern education has been one of the major factors in producing this, since it brings the whole of the younger generation under the same influences and ideas during the most impressionable period of their lives. Here in the United States people should be well aware of this, for the American sociologists, like Robert Lynd and David Riesman, have done more than any others to describe and diagnose this state of affairs.

Now the problem is that while culture and society are unitary, *religion* is pluralistic, most of all perhaps in the United States, and this makes it exceedingly difficult for any particular religion like Catholicism to stand out against the pervasive and overwhelming pressure of the "common way of life." This is why the problem of Christian culture is of such paramount importance, for unless Christians are able to defend their cultural traditions they will not be able to survive. It is necessary to show not only the dangers to human values inherent in our modern unitary culture, but also the positive values of the Christian cultural tradition and its universal significance.

Thus a realistic approach to the problem demands first and foremost a clear recognition of the contradiction and conflict between our unitary culture and our Christian tradition. For in this unitary culture there is little room for the concepts which are fundamental to the Catholic or Christian view—the supernatural, spiritual authority, God and the soul—in fact, the whole notion of the transcendent. So unless students can learn something of Christian culture as a whole—the world of Christian thought and the Christian way of life and the norms of the

Christian community—they are placed in a position of cultural estrangement—the social inferiority of the ghetto without its old self-containedness and self-sufficiency.

To meet this situation it is necessary to make the student aware of the relativity of culture. Today, no less than in the past, the uneducated man accepts the culture in which he lives as culture in the absolute sense. It needs a considerable amount of study and imagination to understand the difference of cultures and the existence and value of other ways of life which diverge from the dominant pattern.

In this respect the position of modern American education is very paradoxical. On the one hand, as I said at the beginning of the chapter, the dominant tendency of American society is towards social conformity, and public education has strengthened this tendency by its uncritical attitude towards "the American Way of Life" and the current democratic ideology. But on the other hand the Americans have had exceptional opportunities to understand the diversity of culture, owing not only to the differences of their own cultural origins, but also to the fact that from the beginning of American history they have been brought into contact with native American peoples who followed a completely different way of life. It has been the American anthropologists who have led the way in the study of these different ways of life and who also were, I believe, the first to formulate the concept of *culture* as the fundamental object of scientific social study.

This concept has been defined by Margaret Mead as "an abstraction from the body of learned behavior which a group of people who share the same tradition transmit entire to their children and in part to those immigrants who become members of the society. It covers not only the arts and the sciences, religions and philosophies to which the word 'culture' has been historically applied, but also the systems of technology, the political practices, the small intimate habits of daily life, such as the way of preparing or eating food or of hushing a child to sleep, as well as the method of electing a prime minister or changing the constitution."[1] And she goes on to say that it has been shown by the experience of anthropologists that all this is a related whole, so that any change in one part of the field will be accompanied by changes in other parts.

Now it is obvious that this concept of culture is not confined to the primitive societies with which anthropologists are chiefly concerned. It is equally applicable to all historic societies, although its study has been divided among several different academic disciplines. Thus the study of primitive societies is the province of the anthropologists, that of modern societies is usually known as sociology and that of the literate societies of the past is the province of the historians, although in each case it is the culture of a society which is the central object of study. This is less obvious in the case of history, owing to the complications introduced by the wider extension of civilized societies and the opportunities for culture contact and conflict. An anthropologist can study the culture of a primitive tribe as an isolated whole, but the historian may have to deal with a whole series of related cultures, extending from the region to the nation and from the nation to the civilization.

It is obvious that the civilization, which in Arnold Toynbee's words is the entity which forms the highest intelligible field of study and which may be almost world-wide in extent, is something very different from the isolated cultural atom which is a

[1] *Cultural Patterns and Technical Change* (New York, Mentor Books, 1955), pp. 12-13.

primitive society. It may be described as a *superculture,* since it may dominate and absorb any number of these primary cultural units. Nevertheless it resembles the primitive culture inasmuch as it is also a *way of life:* it possesses common values, common standards of conduct and common rules of behavior, all of which contribute to the formation of that common moral order which is the essence of cultural unity.

This definition of culture as essentially a moral order is one which should prove equally acceptable to the social anthropologist, the historian and the theologian. For it will cover on the one hand the sociological concept of mores and folkways which has been so influential in American social anthropology, and on the other, the idea of a spiritual community, a community of moral values and ideals which explains the religious or ideological unity of the great world civilizations. Moreover, it will allow us to study the spiritual and intellectual manifestations of a culture as an expression of its fundamental values, as the anthropologists recognize in their study of Pueblo religion and Orokolo drama, and so on. The higher the culture, the more important are its intellectual and spiritual elements, so that the two uses of the word *culture* become almost indistinguishable; i.e., classical culture in the humanist sense is a part of the study of Graeco-Roman culture in the sociological or anthropological sense. This no doubt produces great complications, but then the study of higher cultures is inevitably a complicated matter.

The great world cultures, like China and India and Islam, are classical examples of such a moral order. Each of them possesses or possessed a sacred law and system of values on which its social life was founded.

The Western world today no longer possesses this principle of moral order. It has become so deeply secularized that it no longer recognizes any common system of spiritual values, while its philosophers have tended to isolate the moral concept from its cultural context and have attempted to create an abstract subjective system of pure ethics. If this were all, we should be forced to conclude that modern Western society does not possess a civilization, but only a technological order resting on a moral vacuum.

But Western society inherits the tradition of one of the greatest of the civilizations in the world, and in so far as one recognizes this bond we are still civilized and it is still possible to restore moral order by a return to the spiritual principles on which our Christian civilization was based.

We have shown in the earlier chapters of this book how the essential function of education is "enculturation," or the transmission of the tradition of culture, and therefore it seems clear that the Christian college must be the cornerstone of any attempt to rebuild the order of Western civilization. In order to free the mind from its dependence on the conformist patterns of modern secular society, it is necessary to view the cultural situation as a whole and to see the Christian way of life not as a number of isolated precepts imposed by ecclesiastical authority, but as a cosmos of spiritual relations embracing heaven and earth and uniting the order of social and moral life with the order of divine grace.

Christian culture is the Christian way of life. As the Church is the extension of the Incarnation, so Christian culture is the embodiment of Christianity in social institutions and patterns of life and behavior. It is the nature of Christianity to act as a leaven in the world and to transform human nature by a new principle of divine life.

The Christian culture historian studies this leavening process on the sociological plane. He is concerned not so much with the inner nature of the Christian way of life as with its external expression. Not that the two can be completely separated, any more than we can separate the performance of the liturgy from the spirit of prayer or from the sacraments. For Christian culture is both sacramental and liturgical, as we see so clearly in the history of Christian art.

On the other hand, the student of Christian culture is also concerned with the human material which is subjected to the leavening process. And this material already possesses cultural form, so that the student of Christian culture is also obliged to study the pre-Christian or non-Christian cultures with which it is intermingled. Thus he has three levels or fields of study: (1) The Christian way of life, which is the field of study that he shares with the theologian. (2) The pre-existing or coexisting forms of human culture, which is the field which he shares with the anthropologist and the historian. And (3) the interaction of the two which produces the concrete historical reality of Christendom or Christian culture, which is his own specific field of study.

Christendom, the historical reality of Christian culture as a world movement, was created by the conversion of Hellenistic Roman culture to Christianity and its diffusion to the peoples of the West. To use my terminology, it was a "superculture" which absorbed and overlaid a large number of cultures of various degrees of importance. In the course of ages it has passed through many phases and influenced the development of many different peoples. It has inherited the sacred learning of the Hebrews and the wisdom of the Greeks and law of Rome and has united them in a new unity. It has created new spiritual ideals and new philosophies and new arts and new social institutions. But throughout the course of its history, it has preserved the unity of the Christian faith and the community of the Christian people.

Christian education today is the bearer of this millennial tradition and possesses all the treasures of three thousand years of spiritual creativity. But it exists, as it were, on sufferance in the midst of a predominantly non-Christian order. It must find new channels of expression in this new world and a new approach to the new peoples who do not share the common tradition of the Christian past but who have been forced willy-nilly to partake in the technological order and moral confusion of the modern world.

In one third of the world Christian education is now outlawed by an exclusive totalitarian ideology, in one third it is looked on askance as the organ of Western colonialism and imperialism. In the remaining third it is still free to operate, but, as I say, on sufferance, as the unfashionable hobby of an unprivileged minority. Under these conditions the Catholic scholar may decide to ignore the secular culture that surrounds him and concentrate his whole attention on the Christian culture of the past when the whole of life was governed by religious principles, and art and architecture and philosophy existed to serve the Church. But by doing so, he creates a kind of Christian ghetto, so that a Catholic college might come to resemble those Talmud colleges (Yeshiboth) of nineteenth-century Poland where the student was entirely absorbed in the Jewish sacred tradition without any contact with the Gentile world in which he lived.

On the other hand, the need to compete successfully with the dominant secular education may lead him to sacrifice the study of Christian culture to the modern curriculum of studies, so that the Catholic college comes to provide merely an alternative system of secular education under a denominational label. This is an absurd solution, since the only justification for a minority education is that the minority has something of value to communicate which is not to be found elsewhere. In the case of Christian education it should be unnecessary to insist upon this, since no one can question either the importance of Christian teaching for Christians or the historical importance of Christian culture as the formative influence in the development of Western civilization.

In spite of this, one does encounter a widespread indifference to the subject which is not confined to those who are openly hostile to Christianity. Educated people who are relatively well-informed in history and literature and art are often astonishingly ignorant about the religion to which they profess to belong. And this is the more surprising when a serious effort is being made in Western universities to understand the religions and cultures of the non-European world.

If this process were to continue unchecked, it would mean that Western man would acquire a position of cultural inferiority. He would become more conscious of the spiritual values of other cultures while regarding Western culture as a technological order without moral values or spiritual foundations. It is vital to the survival of the West that we should recover some sense of our moral values and some knowledge of the spiritual tradition of Western Christian culture. The way to do this is by education, and specifically by making the study of Christian culture an integral part of our educational system, which is theoretically directed to this very end. But it is also important for non-Catholics, since they are the heirs of the same tradition of culture, although they may no longer be aware of its relevance to the present crisis of Western society under the external pressure of totalitarian ideologies and the dissolvent forces of secularist materialism.

What is needed is a reorientation of higher studies with the concept of Christian culture as the integrating factor—a new system of humanist studies orientated towards Christian culture rather than classical culture in the old style or the contemporary Western secular culture in the new style.

How is this to be reconciled, on the one hand, with the traditional primacy of classical studies, and on the other, with the insistent claims of modern science and technology and vocational training, not to speak of the study of contemporary history and literature and politics?

Clearly it must not be exclusive. No higher education can be complete without it, but there can be no question of making a clean sweep of the existing curricula and confining the student to the study of the Christian past. It is a question of adjustment which must be solved in different ways in different places according to the needs and opportunities of the particular society and institution.

The situation is not unlike that which the non-Catholic colleges have to face in so far as they try to combine a general study of "Western civilization" with the special studies of the particular student, and the same methods can be applied to the study of Christian culture. Moreover it might be possible to give different courses in Christian culture appropriate to the different studies being taken; thus the course could be orientated towards either literature, history, art, the classics, philosophy or theology or education. Alternatively, we can conceive the study of Christian culture as the province of a special institute on the graduate level. Or it might be offered as a field of concentration to the student in his later years of undergraduate study. In this case, it could be co-ordinated with the student's vocational preparation so as to lead, for example, to teaching on the secondary or collegiate level or to postgraduate studies in law.

The planning of such a curriculum must be a co-operative task: the whole subject ought to be discussed by a committee of experts, like those which have planned the Great Books curriculum or the Columbia Contemporary Civilization course. This can only be done by those who know conditions in the American colleges: what the students are capable of assimilating and what the resources of the teaching staff are. Or alternatively, a special institute could be founded to train picked men in the study, in preparation for the time when a more general course of teaching could be inaugurated.

The other point to be emphasized is the sociological character of the subject. It is not just a question of Christian classics and Christian philosophy, it is the whole tradition of Christian life and thought through the course of history. If one can get the educators to understand the existence of Christian culture as a sociological reality, it is simply a question of finding the ways of studying it that will appeal to the American student. But hitherto the difficulty has been that the existence of this sociological reality has not been fully realized. If people do not see that, they will naturally go astray in discussing the curriculum.

Even if it is not practical politics to introduce the study of Christian culture into the present university curriculum, I believe that we ought to keep it in mind as our ultimate goal, for discussion of it will help to clear up many educational problems. But it may also be introduced as a private study for those who have the necessary aptitudes. Indeed, every advance in education has been prepared by a preliminary period in which the pioneers work outside the recognized academic cadres. This was so at the beginning of the European university and in the beginnings of humanism, while today the diffusion of leisure throughout the affluent society offers new opportunities for free intellectual activity.

XII. THE THEOLOGICAL FOUNDATIONS
OF CHRISTIAN CULTURE

During the last two centuries we have all been taught to think in terms of the nation-state. That has been the real working basis of community, and education has become more and more completely nationalized and has been directed to the study of national culture.

But today this social unity is losing its importance. The nation-state as we knew it in the nineteenth century is being dwarfed or swallowed up by the increasing strain of world war and the increasing pressure of gigantic economic organization.

What is to take its place? Is the culture of the future to be built on class loyalty and party ideology, as the Communists believe? Or will there be developed an all-embracing democratic world organization along the lines of UNO or UNESCO? Neither of these meets the needs of the present situation. The former is too narrow and too exclusive, while the latter are too wide, too invertebrate and too lacking in positive spiritual content to afford a satisfactory basis for cultural community.

Yet there still remains the tradition of those great historic world societies that have moulded human civilization for thousands of years and which brought the divided peoples and cultures of the ancient world into communion with one another by the influence of a common spirit, a common moral order and a common religious ideal. These are the world religions which are the largest and most universal social unities that mankind has hitherto known. They are six in number; three in the West— Christendom, Islam and Judaism; and three in the East—Hinduism, Buddhism and Confucianism. Each of them except Judaism is an international society and each has a continuous history of between a thousand and three thousand years. These are the great spiritual highways that have led mankind through history from remote antiquity down to modern times. They have also been the great educational traditions by which the nations have acquired their script, their literatures and their philosophies. To a great extent they have been separate spiritual worlds, but within their several domains each has created a common world of thought and has brought the nations together in spiritual and intellectual fellowship.

It seems impossible for modern civilization to ignore these societies, since they are the greatest cultural societies that mankind has ever known and since they have had a far deeper spiritual influence on the human mind than the secular civilization that has taken their place. For they are strong just where modern civilization is weak—as moral orders and as teachers of spiritual truth.

Nevertheless modern education has neglected them and ignored their fundamental importance, so that the spiritual tradition of the modern world has become dislocated and lost. No doubt it is impossible for anyone to know all of them, since at present they are still strangers to one another and it is difficult to find a common medium of communication. But that is no reason why we should not study our own spiritual tradition, which has been the creator of our own civilization and especially of the higher spiritual values on which we are still morally dependent.

Modern civilization in spite of its immense technical achievement is morally weak and spiritually divided. Science and technology in themselves are morally neutral and do not provide any guiding spiritual principle. They are liable to be used by any *de facto* power which happens to control society, for its own ends. And thus we see at the present time how the resources of science have been used by the totalitarian state as instruments of power, and how the technological order has been applied in the Western democratic world in the service of wealth and the satisfaction of material needs, even though these needs are artificially stimulated by the same economic powers which find their profit in their satisfaction.

Hence the higher intellectual and spiritual activities become increasingly alienated from society and become a potential danger to its stability. For modern society, like all societies, needs some higher spiritual principle of co-ordination to overcome the conflicts between power and morality, between reason and appetite, between technology and humanity and between self-interest and the common good.

This co-ordinating principle was supplied in the past, in all societies and civilizations, by religion, which was the ultimate guarantee of the moral order and the witness to a realm of spiritual values which transcended the world of human passions and interests. Even if we reject the traditional religions and deny the truth of any particular theological system or doctrine as the modern world has done, we have not escaped from the need of some higher principle of co-ordination if our society is to survive.

This is what Comte saw so clearly in the nineteenth century. But his attempt to provide a rational scientific substitute for religion was a dismal failure, as all similar attempts have been. The fact is that the problem is insoluble by purely rational means, since it involves the principle of transcendence which is essentially theological.

It is therefore essential that we should not allow popular anti-theological prejudice to blind us to the vital sociological and psychological functions that religion has fulfilled in world civilization. In our own case Christianity still exists as a living theological and spiritual tradition, but it has been gradually deprived of intellectual and social influence on modern culture. Yet it has something to offer of which modern technological society is in desperate need—namely, a principle of spiritual co-ordination and a principle of unity—and it is in the field of education that this need and its solution can be brought together.

But we must admit that the failure has not been entirely on the secular side. Christians have retained their belief in theological truth, in a transcendent moral order and in a spiritual community. Nevertheless their theoretical acceptance of these principles is not always accompanied by their cultural realization. Modern Christians have all been more or less influenced by the dominant secular conception of culture. Most of us are shockingly ignorant and forgetful of the wealth of our inheritance. Even the well-educated among us are much better instructed—and usually more interested—in modern secular politics and culture than in the tradition of Christian culture.

This is largely the fault of our education, although underlying it there is the great schism which has divided the whole of life into two unequal parts—the common world of secular life and the restricted, specialized sphere occupied by the Church and religion.

In the past, of course, this was not so. In the Middle Ages and in Catholic countries down to the last century, religion played a large part in the common life, and there was a rich popular religious culture that found expression in art and music and in the celebration of local feasts and pilgrimages.

Yet even in the past the conscious development of lay culture was in a secular direction, and the schism already existed. It is usual to blame the Renaissance and the one-sided development of classical studies for this state of things, but these are responsible only in part. The basic cause seems rather to be found in the medieval tendency to make study a monopoly of the clergy, so that the layman had no place in the medieval university and in the organization of higher scholarship. Hence the rise of a new lay educated class brought with it an independent ideal of lay culture. The consequent division of culture into two halves corresponded to the social division between clergy and laity. While the clergy studied the Bible and the Fathers, the laity studied the classics; while the clergy studied the history of the Church, the laity studied the history of the State; while the clergy studied the traditional Christian philosophy, the laity studied the philosophers of pagan antiquity and the new natural sciences. No doubt the division was not so sharp and schematic as this, but it did undoubtedly lead to an increasing neglect of the traditional culture as a whole by the laity. And when we remember how for the last four hundred years the sphere of lay education has been steadily widening, and that of clerical education has been narrowing, it is difficult to exaggerate the effects of this division on the secularization of modern civilization.

What is needed, therefore, is nothing less than a radical reform of Christian education: an intellectual revolution which will restore the internal unity of Christian culture. It may be impossible to bring about such a change in our lifetime, for educational institutions and curricula are very resistant to change. But since the traditional humanist education is in any case being destroyed in favor of a new scientific model, Christians will have to take positive action to save what they have got, so we should be wise to work for a real restoration of Christian culture rather than merely to fight a defensive action in a purely conservative spirit.

The first essential, the one which can be secured without any drastic change of institutions or laws, is the restoration of a consciousness of the community of Christian culture as the basis of European history and the background of our own particular national and local traditions.

The idea of a Christian culture involves a more comprehensive and realistic conception of Christian society than we are accustomed to. We have to recover the idea of "Christian people" as a true world society of which Israel was the shadow and the antitype; no mere ecclesiastical organization but the organ of a new humanity. This conception is expressed in the early Christian idea of "The Third Race" and more superficially in the medieval idea of Christendom. It finds its classical and authoritative formulation in the Catholic liturgy, especially in that of Easter and Pentecost. On the whole, however, as a result of the narrowing of Christian culture since the Reformation by sectarianism and secularism, we have lost sight of the idea of a Christian people. Not that the sects were unconscious of its importance in principle—indeed the most extreme of them, like the Anabaptists or the Quakers, often emphasized the idea most strongly. But in fact sectarianism destroys it as effectively as secularism, so that ultimately Catholicism itself becomes in the eyes of the world nothing but an exceptionally large and exclusive sect.

It is essential above all to recover the traditional Christian conception of history: first, the doctrine of the transformation and re-creation of humanity in the Incarnation; secondly, the traditional Christian theory of the successive world ages as progressive stages of revelation; thirdly, the ideal of the expansion of the Kingdom of God by the incorporation of the nations in the Kingdom and the enrichment of the Christian tradition by the various contributions of different national cultures and traditions; fourthly, in relation to this, the idea of a providential preparation through which all the positive elements in the pre-Christian and non-Christian world find their fulfillment in the Kingdom of God.

Owing to the separation of ecclesiastical and political history, there has hitherto been no comprehensive study of Christian culture as the historical, though partial, realization in history of these key ideas. The immense wealth of Christian culture as a living world tradition has not been realized except by the specialists who have utilized some part of it for their own ends.

Moreover, this wealth of material is itself a serious obstacle. If the body of Christian literature were no larger than that of classical Greece it would have been studied as a whole, as the classics have been. But in spite of this, I believe the study of Christian culture as a whole is quite possible; there are already a certain number of books which make some approach to the kind of comprehensive treatment that is needed.

It may be objected that the study of Christian culture is unsuited to present-day needs because it will distract the minds of the students from the study of contemporary culture and tend to immerse them in the contemplation of the past—or worse still, in the idealization of limited sections of the past. But the essence of this study, as I envisage it, is that it concerns itself with a dynamic process which does not belong to any single period, but is co-extensive with the history of Christianity and inseparable from it. This process involves three successive phases: (1) the confrontation of Christianity—the Church and the Gospel—with a non-Christian secular or pagan environment; (2) the process of permeation of one by the other; (3) the eventual creation of new forms of culture and thought—art, literature, institutions, and so forth—from the process of interaction.

We can study these three phases in relation to the whole civilizations, e.g., the conversion of the ancient world and the rise of the Byzantine culture; or in relation to particular peoples, e.g., the conversion of the Anglo-Saxons and the rise of Old English Christian culture; or in relation to particular areas of culture, as in the case of the contact and interaction of Christian theology and Greek philosophy and the rise of the Christian-Aristotelian scholastic philosophy; or in relation to particular institutions.

This process is not necessarily confined to any particular period; in principle we could study it with reference to the impact of Catholicism on modern American culture, but such a study would be difficult owing to the fact that we can see only the early stages of the process and we do not know what the eventual product may be. It is necessary to examine the past in order to understand the present and the future; so that the comparative study of Christian culture is very relevant to modern problems and modern needs.

It would be possible to make an extended study of Christian cultures in terms of the Gospel parable of the sower and the seed, showing the cultural correlatives to each of the several alternatives it describes. For the development of Christian culture and Christianity's progress in the individual soul are in many ways parallel. The history of Christianity is essentially that of the extension of the Incarnation; and the study of culture shows the same process at work in history that may be seen in detail in the lives of men.

The whole process creates a religious unity which provides a living spiritual bond of community and possesses a tradition of culture richer and deeper than that of national societies, even though it has been weakened and undermined by centuries of secularism.

Christianity is a real world society which differs from political societies in that it transcends time. The bond of membership is not destroyed by death. It is a world society which unites ages as well as nations. We believe that the men who died for the faith in third-century Rome or seventeenth-century Japan are still partners in the common struggle, no less than those who are leaders of Christian thought and action in our own days.

PART THREE

WESTERN MAN AND THE TECHNOLOGICAL ORDER

XIII. THE RELIGIOUS VACUUM
IN MODERN CULTURE

The predicament in which the world finds itself today is due essentially to two factors: first to the acute secularization of Western culture and secondly to the revolt of the rest of the world against it. For more than two centuries Western civilization has been losing contact with the religious traditions on which it was originally founded and devoting all its energies to the conquest and organization of the world by economic and scientific techniques; and for the last fifty years there has been a growing resistance to this exploitation by the rest of the world —a resistance which has now culminated in a revolt which threatens the very existence of Western society.

Nevertheless this revolt is not directed against the process of secularization itself. It is not a question of a conflict between Western materialism and Oriental spirituality. On the contrary, the East is following the example of the West in its revolt against religious tradition and is going even farther in the direction of the total secularization of culture. It may attack the West as the embodiment of economic exploitation, but it cannot object to its materialism, since the basis of its protest rests on the doctrine of economic materialism which it has borrowed from the West.

Where, then, does Catholicism stand in relation to this situation? In so far as both parties represent rival forms of secularism, it might seem as though Catholicism was not concerned with either of them, so that it could look upon the conflict in the same spirit as the Hebrew prophets regarded the mutual destruction of the world empires in the age of Nebuchadnezzar.

But this is far too simplified a view of the situation. Catholicism has been so deeply involved in the history of Western civilization for the last fifteen hundred years that Catholics cannot regard Europe in the same ways as the Jews regarded the Gentile world. Even today after the Reformation and the Revolution and the secularization of the modern state and modern culture, our society remains in a certain sense Christian.

But we cannot afford to be optimistic. During the last fifty years the new forces that have arisen in the modern world have been openly anti-Christian ones, and the creation of the totalitarian state in Nazi Germany and in Communist Russia produced a new type of religious persecution which is more subtle and far-reaching than anything that the Church has had to face in the past. It is true that the Communist threat is directed against Western culture as a whole as well as against Christianity. But that does not mean that Western culture has become the conscious defender of the Christian faith and of Christian moral values. On the contrary, there has been a serious slump in the practice of religion during the last fifty years in England, and perhaps in Western Europe as a whole. For in order to understand the religious state of the modern world, we must recognize the existence of two contrary tendencies. On the one hand the standards of the religious minority have been steadily rising, while at the same time the general level of religious practice among the majority of nominal Christians or semi-Christians has been rapidly sinking. Therefore the general over-all tendency is for modern Western society to become increasingly pagan, while at the same time Christianity considered as a minority religion retains and perhaps even increases its vitality and its internal strength.

The situation in England is well illustrated in the survey of *English Life and Leisure* which was published in 1951 by B. S. Rowntree and G. R. Lavers. It devotes a good deal of attention to the religious question and makes the first serious attempt to estimate by methods of social survey what influence Christianity exerts in the lives of people today.

The more detailed individual studies and case histories in the survey give the impression that the real cause of modern irreligion is not intellectual, nor is it due to the influence of Communism and dogmatic anti-Christianity. It is sheer indifference: the practical paganism of people who have never thought deeply on this subject, or perhaps on any subject, and who cannot see that Christianity has any relevance to their actual lives.

Here are a few typical extracts from the two hundred case histories. Number 3 "is not a church-goer although she has no objection in principle." She merely says, "It's kids' stuff, but if people are so dumb as to swallow it, it's O.K. by me." Number 24 is not interested in religion. She says if saying her prayers would get her a house, she would say them, but everyone knows it's all nonsense. Number 26 is not interested in religion and her sole knowledge of the Christian doctrine is that "at school we used to read aloud from the Bible—one verse in turn around the class. I once went to church with my friend, but it was all bobbing up and down and I couldn't find my place in the book."

Number 34 is entirely indifferent to religion and says he has traveled too much and seen too much of different religions to believe there is such a thing as a true religion. "Religion only means custom."

Number 49 is profoundly contemptuous of religion. "What do these silly old parsons know about it? Can you pay the rates with prayers? I've no time for their sort of talk. I'd like to set them all to work in the mines."

Number 72 never goes to church because he was fed up with the church when he was in the army, but in his words, "Mind you, religion's a fine thing if you don't have too much of it." He used to send his children to Sunday school to get them out of the house.

Number 97 has absolutely no religious beliefs and thinks that going to church or not is just like going to the cinema. "It's a matter of what suits you." Number 111 has no religious faith. "Not an atheist, you know; I just don't bother. I like the boys to go to church because they ought to know their way around the church services. They look such fools if they don't, if they ever have to go to church."

Now this attitude of contemptuous indifference seems to represent the opinion of the majority among the two hundred cases examined. There is, of course, a considerable minority who take an entirely different view and to whom Christianity is still a living reality. There is a much smaller minority of actively hostile unbelievers including two or three Communists and a few semi-Communists. But each of these seems to be an exceptional type. The real threat to Christianity and also to the future of Western culture, as shown in this survey, is not the rational hostility of a determined minority, but the existence of a great mass of opinion which is not anti-religious but sub-religious, so that it is no longer conscious of any spiritual need for Christianity to fulfill.

This is largely a new situation. For in the past a low level of culture did not necessarily involve a lack of religious belief.

Christianity originally made its strongest appeal to the poor, the uneducated and the socially disinherited: while even the primitive peoples who are the lowest in the scale of material culture have never shown themselves entirely devoid of religious sense.

What is the explanation of this change? I believe it is due above all to the artificial character of modern culture, which is unlike anything that previous ages have experienced. Our modern Western secularized culture is a kind of hothouse growth. On the one hand, man is sheltered from the direct impact of reality, while on the other he is subjected to a growing pressure which makes for social conformity. He seldom has to think for himself or make vital decisions. His whole life is spent inside highly organized artificial units—factory, trade union, office, civil service, party—and his success or failure depends on his relations with this organization. If the Church were one of these compulsory organizations modern man would be religious, but since it is voluntary, and makes demands on his spare time, it is felt to be superfluous and unnecessary.

How are Christians to overcome this difficulty? The answer is not an easy one, for the problem of the conversion of the sub-religious is not unlike the problem of the education of the subnormal. The only real solution is to change the cultural environment which has made it possible for this unnatural state of things to develop. For the sub-religious is also in a certain sense the subhuman, and the fact that apparently healthy and normal individuals can become dehumanized in this way shows that there is something seriously wrong in the society and culture that have made them what they are.

It is a milder form of the same malady which has produced such shocking results in the totalitarian states. In recent years we have often been forced to ask the question how the average well-meaning and well-behaved German or Russian accepted the existence of the concentration camps and the mass purges which have so shocked our humanitarian instincts. And the answer is that the instinct of social conformity is stronger than the instinct of humanitarianism. When the state decides that inhuman measures are required for the good of the party, the individual accepts its decision without criticism and in fact without recognizing what the state is doing.

In Western society this is fortunately still impossible. The state and society as well as the individual still accept humanitarian principles as a matter of faith. But where humanitarian principles are not involved, there is the same tendency to subordinate the moral law and still more the higher truths of religious faith to social conformity and social convenience. Nevertheless I do not think that even the secular humanitarian himself can regard this state of things as a satisfactory one. For the contemporary indifference to religion is accompanied by an indifference to many other things which are necessary for the welfare of society. It is essentially a negative attitude which implies the absence of any deep moral conviction and of any effective social dynamics beyond the appeal to self-interest. It is a sort of spiritual vacuum, which can produce no cultural fruit whatever. In this respect it is inferior even to Communism, which has a dynamic character, even though in the last resort its dynamism is that desire for power which is embodied in the party dictatorships and the police state. And this is one of the greatest of the dangers that threaten the existence of Western culture when the latter is identified with what we call "the democratic way of life." It produces a society which is spiritually neutral and passive, and consequently it affords an easy prey for any strong, aggressive revolutionary power like Communism.

Now it is not the business of Christianity to defend our secularized Western culture from the menace of social or political revolution. From the Christian point of view there is not much to choose between passive agnosticism or indifferentism and active materialism. In fact, both of them may be different symptoms or phases of the same spiritual disease. What is vital is to recover the moral and spiritual foundations on which the lives of both the individual and the culture depend: to bring home to the average man that religion is not a pious fiction which has nothing to do with the facts of life, but that it is concerned with realities, that it is in fact the pathway to reality and the law of life. This is no easy task, since a completely secularized culture is a world of make-believe in which the figures of the cinema and the cartoon-strip appear more real than the figures of the Gospel; in which the artificial cycle of wage earning and spending has divorced men from their direct contact with the life of the earth and its natural cycle of labor and harvest; and in which even birth and death and sickness and poverty no longer bring men face to face with ultimate realities, but only bring them into closer dependence on the state and its bureaucracy so that every human need can be met by filling in the appropriate form.

In such a world there still remains one great social and spiritual institution which is the visible embodiment of divine authority and supernatural truth. So long as the Catholic Church is free to lead its own life and to show in its life and teaching the truth for which it stands, it is bound to make an impression on society, however secularized the culture of the latter has become. But if the gap between the Church and secular culture becomes so wide that there is no longer any means of communication or possibility of mutual understanding between them, then there is a danger that the reaction to the Church may be one of repulsion rather than attraction. And so it is not enough for Catholics to maintain a high standard of religious practice within the Catholic community, it is also necessary for them to build a bridge of understanding out into secular culture and to act as interpreters of the Christian faith to the world outside the Church. This work is not limited to direct missionary activity and religious propaganda in the formal sense. It is the business of every Catholic and especially of every educated Catholic.

We see in the past, especially on the Continent in the nineteenth century, that the secularization of Western culture was not the fault of the clergy and the religious orders, which did their work well, but to the failure and passivity of the Catholic laity, who allowed the case for Christianity to go by default and abandoned the field of higher education to the secularists.

Yet however sub-religious and lacking in spiritual culture and awareness modern society may be, it has a real, if rather foggy, respect for education, and its chief criticisms of orthodox religion are that Christianity is out of date, that the Church takes up a reactionary and obscurantist attitude to modern science and sociology, and that Christians are out of touch with modern thought. Consequently any Catholic who is intellectually alive and is at the same time obviously convinced of the truth of his religion administers a shock to their preconceived ideas. He is not likely to convert them, but he shakes their confidence in the inevitability of the secularist outlook and in the stupidity of the religious view of life.

This is the first step, and small as it is, it is of vital importance.

The second step comes when men become aware of the objective value and importance of religious knowledge: when they realize that such knowledge is no less important for human welfare and for the understanding of reality than economics and the science of nature. This step is still below the threshold of Christianity; it only leads to a point which is common to all the world religions and to many thinkers who have no religious faith, men such as Matthew Arnold in the nineteenth century and George Santayana in our own age. Nevertheless when this step is taken the turning point has been reached.

The existence of a completely secularized culture and of the sub-religious type of humanity rests on the assumption that religious knowledge is no knowledge and that the only real knowledge is concerned with material things and with man's economic needs. And the moment man becomes aware that he stands on the threshold of a spiritual world which is as real as the material world and is in some degree accessible to his mind, his feet are set on the road which leads to the acceptance of the Christian faith and to membership in the Catholic Church. But he cannot follow this path unless Catholics play their part as interpreters and communicators.

How can this be done? The present situation is that modern secularized culture has become a closed world and has lost all contact with the higher world of spiritual reality. In the past this higher world was rendered intelligible and visible to Western man through the medium of Christian culture, which provided a whole series of ways of approach adapted to the different types of mind and the different forms of intellectual activity. Today all these avenues have become closed by ignorance, prejudice or neglect, and they have to be re-opened by the spiritual and intellectual action of Catholics, each working in his own field towards the common end, and it is here the work of the educated Catholic is of such importance. There is an apostolate of study as well as an apostolate of action and of prayer.

Christian culture is not the same thing as the Christian faith. But it is only through the medium of culture that the Faith can penetrate civilization and transform the thought and ideology of modern society. A Christian culture is a culture which is orientated to supernatural ends and spiritual reality, just as a secularized culture is one which is orientated to material reality and to the satisfaction of man's material needs. This is the basic conflict on which St. Augustine founded his philosophy of history. In his view the dynamic principle of society is the common will or psychological drive. Therefore the only dynamic principle in a human society which is godless and self-centered is the will to self-satisfaction—*cupiditas*—whether that is the competitive impulse of selfish acquisitiveness, or the mass impulses of class conflict and the will to power on the part of states and nations.

But against this tendency of man to create a self-centered, closed world which is ultimately doomed to self-destruction by its own destructive instincts, there is the divine process of spiritual restoration and reintegration which finds its center in the Incarnation and its orbit in the Christian faith. With Christianity a new dynamic principle enters the life of humanity and reorganizes it round a new spiritual center and towards a new supernatural end. This principle is social as well as individual. It is embodied in the life of an organized community—the Catholic Church—and it extends its influence to every aspect of human life and every form of social activity. The elements of human society—family, economic association, city and state—remain the same, but in proportion as they come under the influence of the higher spiritual order, they are directed to new ends.

Thus the contribution of Christianity to culture is not merely the addition of a new religious element; it is the process of re-creation which transforms the whole character of the social organism. It breaks down the closed, self-centered world of secularist culture and gives human society a new spiritual purpose which transcends the conflicting interests of individual and class and race. Thus it provides the psychological motive for the creation of a genuinely universal culture from which no class or race is excluded.

No doubt the Christian solution at first sight appears imperfect as compared with the secular ideologies and utopias which offer men everything at once on condition that they submit themselves totally to their control. In fact, however, these ideologies only increase the social divisions and conflicts of the modern world and, instead of creating a utopia, they only plunge mankind deeper and deeper into slavery and war.

Christianity, on the other hand, offers no immediate panacea for the complex malady of the modern world. It has eternity before it, and it can afford to take its time. But for that very reason a Christian culture is potentially far wider and more catholic than a secular one. It is God-centered, not man-centered, and it consequently changes the whole pattern of human life by setting it in a new perspective.

Philosophy and science, history and literature, all acquire a new character and become deepened and widened when they are seen in this perspective. That is why the Christian culture of the past saw theology as the queen of the sciences. The extension of the field of the sciences by the growth of knowledge also brings new opportunities for widening the range of Christian culture. Every advance of this kind, however small, makes the Faith more accessible and intelligible to the modern world. We may not be able to build cathedrals like the Catholics of the thirteenth century, or write epics like Dante, but we can all do something to make man conscious of the existence of religious truth and the relevance of Catholic thought, and to let the light into the dark world of a closed secularist culture.

XIV. AMERICAN CULTURE AND THE
LIBERAL IDEOLOGY

In the previous chapter I have discussed the predicament of the modern Western world—a world which has been increasingly detached from its spiritual roots in Christian culture but which has at the same time advanced in material and scientific power, so that it has extended its influence over the rest of the world until it has created a cosmopolitan technological world order. But this world order possesses no spiritual foundation and appears to the ancient civilizations of the East and the new peoples of Africa as a vast organization of material power which has been created to serve the selfish greed for power of Western man—hence the revolt of Asia and Africa against the West which now threatens the peace and stability of the world.

Now the United States occupy an anomalous position in this conflict. They have always taken a leading part in the development of technocracy and in the economic expansion of the West, so that the non-European peoples regard them as the foremost and most typical representatives of Western materialism and economic imperialism. Yet they have never taken a prominent part in the colonial movement. They have from the beginning been hostile to the spirit of European imperialism and have shown a genuine sympathy with the strivings of subject peoples for freedom and national independence.

Yet in spite of this the American cannot dissociate himself from the fate of Western man. Indeed he is Western man in a more complete and typical way than any European people. It is easy to see why this should be so. The United States achieved their independence in the heyday of the European Enlightenment, and this ideology of the Enlightenment was the foundation of their national existence. The peoples of Europe, in spite of their revolutions, were committed to the past and to their separate national traditions. But Americans were committed to the future. They saw the Revolution as the dawn of a new age and a new civilization which was destined to be the civilization of a new world, and consequently the principles of the Constitution and the Declaration of Independence were not transitory and fallible opinions but absolute truths which no citizen could question and which were to remain the firm foundations of the American way of life.

Thus while the ideology of the Enlightenment was common to Europe and America, its impact on the culture was completely different. In Europe it marked the coming of an age of criticism and conflict in which no truth was left unquestioned and the spiritual unity of Western culture was lost. But in America it meant the coming of an age of faith—the establishment of a doctrine which united the whole people in allegiance to certain common truths. The result of this situation was that while the ideas were the same, their relation to the traditional religions of society was entirely different.

In Europe there was a general conflict between Liberalism or the ideology of the Enlightenment and the traditional forms of religion, especially Catholicism, which has divided Latin Europe down to our own days. In America the universal acceptance of the Liberal ideology precluded any such conflict. It was essentially non-controversial and was accepted as common ground by all the different sections of American opinion, whether religious or non-religious. The possession of this common ideological basis has given Americans a strong sense of cultural unity and has made it possible for them to enter the technological era with full confidence in their ability to use the new techniques in the service of the American way of life.

Nevertheless the process of secularization which has accompanied the progress of technology threatens the foundation of American culture no less than the traditional culture of the Old World. The American ideology on which the Constitution was based involved two essential and related concepts—in the first place the philosophy of Natural Law and Natural Rights and secondly the limitation of the power of the state which left the individual citizen free to lead his own life and organize his economic and cultural activities.

According to the old American system, the state or states were concerned with the preservation of law and order and national independence. Everything else—religion, education and economic life—was the sphere of free individual action in which the state had no voice. All this has been changed in the last hundred years by inevitable historical forces.

The *State*, that unitary authoritative bureaucratic power, against which the American Revolution was a protest, has returned armed with new powers of supervision and psychological control of which George III never dreamed, while technology has unified the economic life of the nation into a vast system of organization in which every individual has his allotted place.

In the new America the socialization and secularization of education has created an immense professionalized organ for the creation of moral and intellectual uniformity. In this way the constitutional principle of the separateness of Church and State which was intended to secure religious freedom has become the means of secularizing the American mind so that the churches have lost all control over the religious formation of the people. This was not so in the earlier phase of American history when the churches were the chief, and often the only, organs of education and culture.

The American way of life was built on a threefold tradition of freedom—political, economic and religious—and if the new secularist forces were to subjugate these freedoms to a monolithic technological order, it would destroy the foundations on which American culture was based. The American way of life can only maintain its character within the general framework of Western Christian culture. If this relation is lost, something essential to the life of the nation will be lost and American democracy itself will become subordinated to the technological order.

The American people as a whole are dimly aware of this. The open profession of a secularist ideology which I described in the last chapter is no longer common in the United States. On the contrary, there has been a remarkable increase in church membership and church attendance during recent years. This has been prompted, I think, not by any deep religious change, but rather by a spirit of social conformity and a feeling that religion is in some way a vital part of the American way of life. But this is not enough. It does not involve any real understanding of the nature of Christian culture and it has not affected the predominantly secular character of American education and intellectual life.

The only sections of the American population that are fully

committed to maintaining full Christian education are the Catholics, and they are not usually regarded as the typical representatives of the American tradition. Nevertheless in this matter they stand for a principle which was an integral part of the old American heritage, and in so doing they are defending something which should be the common concern of all the American churches.

It is therefore important that the study of Christian culture in the American Catholic college should not confine itself to the Christian culture of Europe but should devote special attention to the problem of the Enlightenment and the way in which the doctrines of Natural Law and the theory of the limited state had their original roots in the Christian tradition.

I dealt with this subject in *The Judgment of the Nations*, when in England Catholics and Liberals were forced to stand together against the menace of totalitarianism and when these two principles of Natural Law and the limited or constitutional state were the special object of the totalitarian attack.[1]

Today the attack comes from a different quarter, but it is the same principles that are threatened alike by the Communist ideology, which is totalitarian in the same sense as National Socialism, and by the technological secularism which is the enemy within the Western world and which is equally opposed to these fundamental principles. It is only from the standpoint of a living Christian culture that we can defend these principles that are the common foundation of the Western way of life. In America, however, the sense of a common Christian culture has always been weakened or lost by the strength of the sectarian tradition. Thus, while the beginnings of American cul-

[1] See especially Pt. 1, Chapter 3, on "The Causes of European Disunity" and Pt. 2, Chapter 2, on "Christian Social Principles."

ture, above all in New England, were closely associated with the Christian tradition, it was identified with a very highly specialized and exclusive sectarian tradition; and thereafter every new wave of immigration and colonial settlement was associated with some new manifestation of religious sectarianism. Thus the American pattern of religion and culture was that of a mosaic of sects and churches united only by their common devotion to religious and civic freedom, which became fundamental assumptions of the American Constitution and the American way of life.

When the Catholics came with the mass immigrations of the nineteenth century they were also fitted into this sectarian pattern and accepted the same civic loyalties. But the Catholics have not conformed to the American pattern in one important respect. While the Protestant churches have gradually abandoned the field of culture to the State and have confined their activity to the purely ecclesiastical sphere, the Catholics have continued to assert their rights in the field of education.

The reasons for the general abandonment of religious education by the Protestant churches are complex. On the one hand, it has been due to the fissiparous tendency of American Protestantism and the difficulty of finding a programme that would be equally acceptable to them all, like the Agreed Syllabus which has been adopted in England in recent years. On the other hand, it was due to the fact that public education in America long retained a vaguely Christian character, which satisfied the needs of the Protestant majority. In any case there is no reason to believe that the secularization of education forms any part of the Protestant tradition, and in this matter the Catholics today are standing for a principle which is common to all Christians and which in the past has played an important part in the development of American culture.

If this is so, it is important for Catholic educationalists to take a wide view of their responsibilities and their intellectual task. They have to keep alive the concept of Christian culture in a secular world. It is not enough to maintain a limited course of sectarian instruction. Christian education should be wider, not narrower, than that of the secular school. While the latter initiates the student into the life and thought of modern secular society, Christian education should be an initiation into a universal spiritual society—the community of the *civitas Dei.*

The central purpose of Christian education should be to actualize this citizenship which we all accept as a truth of faith but which should be realized as a membership of a real community, more real than that of nation or state and more universal than secular civilization. It is a community that transcends time so that past and present coexist in a living reality.

The vital problem of Christian education is a sociological one: how to make students culturally conscious of their religion; otherwise they will be divided personalities—with a Christian faith and a pagan culture which contradict one another continually. We have to ask ourselves are we Christians *who happen to live* in England or America, or are we English or Americans who happen to attend a church on Sundays? There is no doubt which is the New Testament view; there the Christians are one people in the full sociological sense, but scattered among different cities and peoples. But today we mostly take the opposite view, so that our national cultures are the only culture we have and our religion has to exist on a sectarian sub-cultural level. Thus the sociological problem of a Christian culture is also the psychological problem of integration and spiritual health. This is the key issue. Even a ghetto culture is preferable to no religious culture at all, but under modern conditions the ghetto solution is no longer really practicable. We must make an effort to achieve an open Christian culture which is sufficiently conscious of the value of its own tradition to be able to meet secularist culture on an equal footing.

In America both the need and opportunity for this are greater than elsewhere. The technological order has been more highly developed than anywhere else in the world, and with it the pressure of secularization has steadily increased. But at the same time America still possesses the priceless advantages of educational and intellectual freedom, so that we are still free to work and plan for the restoration of Christian culture. The opportunity may not be with us for long. For the Catholic schools and colleges, which are the only nation-wide representatives of Christian education, are already regarded as an anomaly, and there are many people who regard them as opposed to the dominant pattern of American society, which is founded on the secular public school and finds its culmination in the State university. At the same time there are few who realize the dangers to human freedom involved in the technological order or who totally reject the spiritual values that we have inherited from the Christian culture of the past. Even among secularists there are many who are concerned with the preservation of spiritual freedom and whose opposition to Christian, and particularly Catholic, education is due to the belief that organized religion is the enemy of freedom, and consequently of the American tradition. It is necessary to clarify the issues and to show how the trend of the modern world towards inhuman totalitarianism demands an alliance of the divided forces of humanism and religion if it is to be mastered.

XV. WESTERN MAN AND THE
TECHNOLOGICAL ORDER

This is the age of Frankenstein, the hero who created a mechanical monster and then found it had got out of control and threatened his own existence. Frankenstein represents our age even more truly than Faust represented the age of Goethe and the romantics. Western man has created the technological order, but he has not discovered how to control it. It is beginning to control him, and if it does, there seems no way of preventing it from destroying him.

Our dilemma is most obvious in the new techniques of warfare. These have become so efficient that they make the path to self-destruction, mass destruction and even world destruction a short and easy one. Yet the technological order offers us no techniques of international relations by which this might be avoided.

In the field of diplomacy and peace and international law, we still have to depend on the older humanistic techniques which are based on the assumption that man is a reasonable being, and consequently they are techniques that can only be applied in exceptionally favorable circumstances. It is as though we were in a ship that was guaranteed to go ten times faster than any other, but which can only be navigated safely in a dead calm.

Today the international waters are as calm as they are ever

likely to be. Yet there is a kind of war existing between Israel and the Arab Republic and between China and Formosa, and nearer home there is only the fragile protection of Señor Castro's sanity standing in the way of a war between Cuba and the U.S.A.

We all realize in our rational moments that the world has become one community, yet all over the world the forces which make the strongest appeal are those racialist and nationalist movements that deny this principle and gladly sacrifice the rest of the world to the interests and passions of their paranoiac group-consciousness. And this applies also to the political ideologies that are non-racial, like communism, at least in its Stalinist form. Indeed one cannot find a more extreme example of this group paranoia than in that extraordinary *History of the Communist Party* for which Stalin was personally responsible.

No doubt it will be said that these things are exceptional and that there is enough sanity in the world to master them, as it mastered Hitler's paranoia—though at what a cost! Unfortunately there seems reason to believe that this disorder permeates the whole of modern civilization and that it exists under the surface or near the surface in our own society and in every society. The more the technological order advances, and the greater the pressure it exerts on the individual, the stronger is the emotional reaction by which the forces that have been suppressed find release. In the pre-technological order, the craftsman and the manual laborer tended to release their psychic tensions in the exercise of their work. But in the technological order this is not so, the man who drives a truck or minds a machine has to subordinate himself to the discipline of the machine. His emotions find no expression in his work—or, if they do, he is a bad workman. They must find an outlet outside his work—in his free time—occasionally by violent action, but more usually by the contemplation of the patterns of violent action that are provided by the mechanized industries that cater for this need. But this is not a real solution. It is only a temporary palliative, and the fundamental emotional needs remain unsatisfied.

But this problem is not only one for the manual worker. It also affects the intellectuals and the specialists without whom the technological order could not be maintained. They also suffer from a sense of frustration and take a gloomy view of the prospects of civilization, as we may see in current literature.

What is the real cause of this failure of humanity to adapt itself to the technological order? Is it a fundamental defect, inherent in the very nature of that order? Or is it simply due to the inevitable slowness of human nature to adapt itself to sudden change?

No doubt the change has been a very sudden one. I myself was born and brought up in a pre-technological order, and I remember it very clearly. But even at that time anyone who could take a broad view of Western civilization could see what was coming, and even in the preceding generation to my own, there were writers such as Nietzsche, who saw the decline of humanist values and of liberal humanist civilization, though he had no inkling of the new techniques that were about to transform human existence.

Nevertheless he pointed out—and so did other thinkers about the same time—that Western culture no longer possessed the spiritual resources which had formerly justified its existence and without which it could not survive, so that the causes of our present predicament were already present in the liberal-humanist culture of the pre-technological period. Indeed the fundamental problem that we have to face had already manifested itself at the end of the eighteenth century.

There has never been a society that was more civilized in the humanist sense than the French society of the Enlightenment, nor one more completely convinced of the powers of reason and science to solve all the problems of life and to create a completely rational culture, based on a firm foundation of science and philosophy. Yet when this society, as represented by Condorcet and his friends, had the opportunity to put their ideas into practice in the first years of the French Revolution, they failed disastrously and were themselves destroyed, almost to a man, by the eruption of the irrational forces that they had released. One of the writers of the emigration has described in a remarkable passage how he came to realize the fallacies of the rationalist ideology in a sudden flash of intuition one night as he was making the terrible march across the frozen Zuyder Zee with the defeated English army in 1796, and how all the illusions of the Enlightenment dropped away from him under the cold light of the winter stars.

And the same disillusionment was experienced, in a less dramatic way, by many of the greatest minds of the age—by William Blake, and Joseph de Maistre and Francisco Goya. The latter is an especially interesting case, for he was himself a disciple of the Enlightenment in his conscious mind. Yet in his later works, he shows in an almost apocalyptic way that historic events are not the work of rational calculation or even of human will. Under the surface of history there are superhuman or subhuman forces at work which drive men and nations before them like leaves before a gale.

But none of this was seen by nineteenth-century Liberalism—

except perhaps by the small group of French theorists, represented by Alexis de Tocqueville. As a rule they continued to follow in the steps of the Enlightenment, as though the debâcle of the Revolution had never occurred. They closed their eyes to realities or concealed the ugly reality with the veils of idealism and romanticism.

It is easy to find excuses for them. The triumph of applied science seemed to justify their faith in reason, and the doctrine of progress was borne out by the expansion of Western trade and industry which were conquering the world. They could not realize how narrow was the ground on which they stood, and how rapidly it was being eroded by the powers of change that they had set in motion.

But in the later part of the nineteenth century there was a reaction against liberalism which found its most striking expression in the new German Empire with its imposing development of military power and its disciplined organization of scientific research that prepared the way for the technological order. Nietzsche was the prophet of this anti-liberal reaction. He expressed the will to power that inspired it, while at the same time he mercilessly exposed its cultural nihilism and its loss of spiritual values.

Yet it was a liberal and a rationalist, Sigmund Freud, writing at Vienna in the early years of the twentieth century, who dealt the final blow to the liberal ideology by his analysis of the psyche and his discovery of the vast uncharted territory of the unconscious. And when they had tasted the fruit of this tree of psychological knowledge, the children of Adam Smith were driven out of their cosy liberal paradise, in which they had lived so securely, into a jungle where they had to face wild beasts whose very existence they had ignored.

Thus at the very moment when man acquired an almost un-limited control over nature by the new technology, he became aware of his own insufficiency. It was impossible to ignore this lesson, for it was brought home to us by the terrible experience of the Second World War and all that preceded it. In Germany and Austria, where the new technology and the new psychol-ogy had originated, we saw not psychopathic individuals, but mass movements and whole peoples surrendering to the forces of the unconscious and sacrificing themselves to the dark gods of racial mythology.

After this experience it is impossible for educated man to return to the old rationalist illusions. We must face the fact that the vast expansion of man's external powers by science and technology which are the creation of human reason have done nothing to strengthen the power of reason in the moral order which is its proper domain. For the moral order and the techno-logical order have become out of gear with one another, and as the technological order has advanced and become stronger, the moral order has grown weaker. The technological order lends itself most easily to the service of the will to power which, as Nietzsche saw, is a fundamentally amoral power, destructive of moral values. It resembles those jinn of whom we read in the Arabian Nights that were ready to do anything, good or bad, in the service of any man who possessed the word of power or the talisman.

Thus we are confronted with a conflict between human nature and civilization which is far more severe than anything that was known in the past, since the technological order in-volves a more far-reaching system of social control and de-mands a much more complete co-ordination of social disciplines which have hitherto enjoyed a considerable measure of independence. Quite apart from any question of ideology, the inner logic and outward efficiency of the system demand total co-ordination and total unity, so that education and science, business and industry, government and public opinion shall all co-operate with one another in a closed organization from which there are no outlets.

Now it is obvious that a system of this kind is entirely opposed to the ideals of eighteenth- and nineteenth-century liberalism which have inspired the growth of modern democracy. It is true that liberalism was never entirely consistent in this respect, for it was economic individualism and free competition of economic liberalism which laid the foundations of the technological order in the new industrial society of the nineteenth century. Nevertheless the liberals believed that the technological servitude of the factory system would be compensated by the advantages of political liberty and popular education, no less than by the growing prosperity of the middle classes who formed the new élite. They were honestly convinced that the conflict between human nature and social injustice would be solved or ameliorated by political liberty and economic progress, and if they were wrong, their optimism, on the whole, was more justifiable than the pessimism of the Marxian Socialists with their theory of the increasing misery of the proletariat.

In the same way the social reformers and the new psychologists were influenced by the same liberal ideals. For the latter believed that the psychological conflicts of the individual were largely soluble by psychological enlightenment and psychological freedom. The more the limits of social control could be pushed back beyond the psychological frontier, the more the personality would be freed from the tyranny of the super-ego and from the repressions and frustrations that it involved.

This was the solution which Freud's earlier writings tended to favor, but in these he was concerned as a psychiatrist only with the problems of the neurotic personality. As a philosopher he was always aware of the necessity for repression or the renunciation of instinctual gratification as a necessary condition of civilization. In fact, as I have pointed out, Freud has done more than any other modern thinker to undermine the liberal ideology by his diagnosis of the psychological fallacies on which its humanitarian and optimistic ethics were based.

The breakdown of liberalism has been followed by the rise of collectivism and the totalitarian state—a development which is closely related to that of the technological order. The strength of the collectivist solution is to be found in its elimination or suppression of every element that can weaken the common purpose or interfere with the smooth running of the economic or political machine. It solved the conflict between human nature and civilization by denying its existence and forcing human nature into conformity with the political and economic pattern by the Procrustean surgery which fits the new man to the new order. It does not attempt to solve the psychological conflicts of the individual, but by denying the validity of the moral values and the moral judgment, it reduces the recalcitrant individual to the position of a criminal or an insane person. Thus the concentration camp provides a final answer to social criticism, just as the lunatic asylum solves the social problems of the psychotic.

The disadvantage of this solution is that it removes the psychological barriers of moral criticism and moral judgment which restrain the pathological development of collective delusions and neuroses. There is no reason to suppose that the ends of the collective will of society or the state will be more rational or more moral than those of the individual. On the contrary, the moral standards of states and governments, especially in times of war and revolution, are usually very much lower than those of the individual. Thus a state which deliberately suppresses moral criticism and makes the will to power its only end is capable of any iniquity, as we have seen in our own life-time, in the man-made hells of Belsen and Auschwitz and in the wholesale proscriptions and purges of Stalin's Russia.

But what is most alarming in these developments is the way in which this reversion to barbarism has been associated with technological advance. Indeed, the new barbarism is itself technological, inasmuch as the whole system of propaganda and persecution, mass trials and concentration camps represents a carefully thought-out technique for ensuring social conformity and remaking mankind after some new ideological pattern.

No wonder that Western man recoils in horror from this degradation of civilization and refuses to admit the possibility of its victory over the free world. Nevertheless the experience of the last thirty years has shown that the modern Western synthesis of political liberalism and economic technocracy involves certain moral weaknesses and contradictions in the system which make it incapable of providing a satisfactory answer to the totalitarian challenge. For while the democratic technological society is free, it lacks the higher moral aims which alone can justify the immense developments of technological power and organization. The system exists primarily to satisfy the material needs and demands of the consumers, and these demands are artificially determined by the advertisers who are the agents of the producers, so that the whole system has a circular movement and feeds upon itself.

The totalitarian state, on the other hand, in spite of its fundamental immorality, is able to impose a relative moral aim on its technology which is planned to serve the common good—the good of the state—rather than the profit of any particular financial or industrial interest. And this sense of a common purpose is a source of moral strength for the individual, even though the state itself has no higher moral aims. Sparta may be no more than a glorified barracks, while Sybaris might be the home of wealth and material culture, yet throughout the Greek world Sparta was idealized and Sybaris was despised, because the Spartan lived by law and was willing to sacrifice everything to the common purpose, while the Sybarite lived for himself and made wealth and pleasure the standards of his life. Hence there is little reason to suppose that in the present world conflict democracy will triumph over communism, if the former represents nothing more than a higher standard of material welfare and an advanced technology subordinated to the satisfaction of material needs and the enrichment of those financial and industrial interests that can most effectively stimulate and satisfy the demands of the consumer.

There is, however, another alternative which has been ignored both by the liberal rationalists who put their trust in individual reason guided by self-interest and by the psychologists who asserted the power of irrational impulses and the politicians and philosophers who exalted the will to power. This alternative is represented by the traditional religious or philosophical doctrine which solves the psychological and moral conflict by reference to a higher order of transcendent truths and values and ends, to which both the life of the individual and that of society are subordinated. The strength of this solution is that it, and it alone, provides a principle of co-ordination, so that the individual is not entirely sacrificed to the community, nor the community to the individual. It is, therefore, psychologically the more "economical" method, whatever may be its metaphysical validity. Without such a principle of co-ordination there is no satisfactory means of reconciling the aims of the ego with the collective will. Indeed there is no room for the collective will itself as a rational force, and one is left with nothing more than some sort of herd instinct which has no reference to anything except the fears and delusions of the mass mind.

We cannot ignore the fact that every civilization from the beginning of history down to modern times has accepted the existence of a transcendent spiritual order of this kind and has regarded it as the ultimate source of moral values and of moral law. And in every high civilization we find a correspondingly high development of this conception. It is difficult to explain this concept as the product of a kind of infantile regression, as the rationalists do,[1] since in every civilization some of the most advanced minds of every age have been devoted to it. Even in cases where the traditional religious beliefs have lost their hold on society, as in ancient Greece, we see how the leaders of thought still remained faithful to it and proceeded to construct elaborate metaphysical systems by which it could be justified.

If this is an illusion, then civilization is also an illusion, for there is an obvious relation between the breakdown of the moral order when it is deprived of its spiritual aims and sanctions and the breakdown of civilization when it loses its relation to the moral order. The reason why modern civilization has been able to secularize itself as it has done, is that the domain of reason has been so widened and strengthened by the development of science and technology that man came to believe that

[1] E.g., S. Freud in *The Future of an Illusion* (1927).

his reason was strong enough to create a self-sufficient moral order which would in turn produce the perfect society. In this he was mistaken, as the experience of the last fifty years has shown us. As Freud pointed out, man was attempting to live beyond his psychological means, an attempt that must lead to bankruptcy sooner or later.

It would seem, therefore, that the only way out of the impasse in which modern civilization finds itself is to return to the old spiritual foundations and restore the old alliance between religion and culture. But is this still possible? Or has the advance of modern science made such an alternative impossible? This was the common idea in the nineteenth century. It was part of the liberal ideology which presupposed the existence of an inevitable movement of progress by which science continually advances and religion continually retreats. But in the first place the existence of irreversible movements of this kind is highly questionable, and in the second place there is no reason to suppose that religion and science are simply alternatives to one another. They are obviously distinct in their nature, their methods, and their aims. They are not mutually exclusive but rather complementary. So that it is possible that the more science a culture has, the more religion it needs.

No doubt they may become exclusive subjectively, owing to the concentration of attention on one field at the expense of the other. This is what actually occurred in modern times when Western culture turned its face away from the spiritual world in order to concentrate its whole energy on the discovery and exploitation of the new world of science and technology. But as soon as men come to realize that this one-sided development of culture has become a threat to its survival and is contrary to the real interests of man and society, there is nothing except habit and prejudice to prevent a return to the principle of spiritual order and a recovery of this lost dimension of Western culture.

As I have said, the human mind has always been conscious of the existence of an order of spiritual values from which its moral values derive their validity. This is also an order of spiritual realities which finds its center in transcendent being and divine truth. All the great religions of the world agree in confessing this truth—that there is an eternal reality beyond the flux of temporal and natural things which is at once the ground of being and the basis of rationality.

The Christian faith goes much further than this. It and it alone shows how this higher reality has entered into human history and changed its course. It shows how a seed of new life was implanted in humanity by the setting apart of a particular people as the channel of revelation which found its fulfillment in the Incarnation of the Divine Word in a particular person at a particular moment of history. It shows how this new life was communicated to a spiritual society which became the organ of the divine action in history, so that the human race may be progressively spiritualized and raised to a higher spiritual plane.

Seen from this angle the modern progress of science and technology acquires a new meaning. The technological order which today threatens spiritual freedom and even human existence by the unlimited powers which it puts at the service of the human passion and will loses all its terrors as soon as it is subordinated to a higher principle. Technology that is freed from the domination of individual self-interest and the mass cult of power would then fall into its place as a providential instrument in the creation of a spiritual order. But this is impossible, so long as our society remains devoid of all spiritual aims and is intent only on the satisfaction of its lust for power and the satisfaction of its selfish desires.

A change can only be brought about by the radical reorientation of culture to spiritual ends. This is an immense task, since it means a reversal of the movement which has dominated Western civilization for the last two or three centuries. Yet such a change has been in the air for a very long time, and it has been predicted or advocated by prophets and poets and philosophers ever since the beginning of the nineteenth century: by the poets, like Blake and Coleridge and Novalis; by the socialists and sociologists, like Comte and Saint-Simon and Bazard; and by philosophers like Nietzsche. All of them were aware of the nature of the problem and the inevitability of a great spiritual change, though they were all blinded by the partiality of their vision—the poets by their rejection of science, the sociologists by their rejection of God, and Nietzsche by his simultaneous rejection of both God and humanity.

The conversion and reorientation of modern culture involves a double process, on the psychological and intellectual levels. First, and above all, it is necessary for Western man to recover the use of his higher spiritual faculties—his powers of contemplation—which have become atrophied by centuries of neglect during which the mind and will of Western man was concentrated on the conquest of power—political, economic and technological. This rediscovery of the spiritual dimension of human existence may be either religious or philosophical: it may be based on some kind of religious conversion through which man realizes his need for God and discovers a new world of spiritual truth and moral values; or it may involve an objective metaphysical recognition of the ontological importance and significance of the spiritual factor. Perhaps it must be both, for the study of the varieties of religious experience in the last two hundred years has shown how little can be achieved by the non-intellectual emotionalism of the revivalist traditions which have been so strong even in a secular environment like that of nineteenth-century America. But a complete change of spiritual orientation cannot be effective unless it takes place on a deep psychological level. It cannot be had for the asking! It can only be reached by a long and painful journey through the wastelands. Meanwhile there is an essential preliminary step which can be taken at once wherever and whenever people can be found who recognize this need for spiritual change.

This is the reform of our system of higher education of which I have spoken at length. In the modern world the average man can go through his whole education without becoming aware of the existence of this elementary and essential spiritual factor either in the individual psyche or in the life of civilization. Whether he studies the liberal arts or science and technology, he is given no inkling of the existence of any higher principle which can be known and which can influence individual behavior or social culture. Yet, as I have said, all the great historic civilizations of the past recognized the existence of some spiritual principles or ends of this kind and made them the key of their interpretation of reality and their concepts of moral order. Hence a system of education like that of the modern secular state which almost totally ignores the spiritual component in human culture and in the human psyche is a blunder so enormous that no advance in scientific method or educational technique is sufficient to compensate for it. In this respect we are inferior to many far less advanced cultures which have retained their consciousness of a spiritual order, for wherever this consciousness exists the culture still possesses a principle of integration.

We have a long way to go before we can recover this lost principle of integration. But it is the function of education to open the mind to an appreciation of the spiritual as well as the scientific and humanistic inheritance of culture. If, as I have suggested, the spiritual vacuum in modern Western culture is a danger to its existence, it is the duty of the educationalist to point this out and to show how this vacuum has been filled in other ages or in other cultures. But the Christian educationalist can do much more than this, since he is fully aware of the reality of the spiritual order and is a living witness to the spiritual values on which our civilization was founded.

No doubt his position is a difficult one, since if he is a teacher in a denominational school or college his work is confined to a small separate world which is hardly aware of the enormous gap which divides its traditional beliefs from the forces that rule the world today; while if he is engaged in public education, he is forced by the conditions of his work to treat vital spiritual issues as lying outside his sphere of competence.

But in spite of all this, he is the one man who is in a position to bridge the gulf between the private world of religious faith and spiritual values and the public world of technology, scientific positivism and social conformism. So long as the Christian tradition of higher education still exists, the victory of secularism even in a modern technological society is not complete. There is still a voice to bear witness to the existence of the forgotten world of spiritual reality in which man has his true being.

SPECIFIC PROGRAMS FOR THE STUDY OF CHRISTIAN CULTURE
by John J. Mulloy[1]

[1] Mr. Mulloy is the editor of the synthesis volume of Christopher Dawson's thought, *The Dynamics of World History*, and has carried on with Mr. Dawson a continuing discussion about the implications of the Christian Culture proposals for the college and university curriculum. Mr. Mulloy teaches Modern European History at Central High School in Philadelphia, lectures in Cultural Anthropology at La Salle College, and serves as chairman of the Committee on Religion in a Free Society, sponsored by the Philadelphia chapter of the National Conference of Christians and Jews for the furtherance of the dialogue and interreligious understanding.

In development of the ideas which he here sets forth for specific programs of Christian culture study, Mr. Mulloy has given graduate courses and conducted faculty seminar discussions in Christian Culture and in the Philosophy of History at Gonzaga University (Spokane, Washington); Rosemont College (Rosemont, Pennsylvania—near Philadelphia); Saint Mary-of-the-Woods College (near Terre Haute, Indiana); Mount St. Mary's College (Los Angeles, California); and St. Norbert College (West De Pere, Wisconsin—near Green Bay). He also served as organizer and general chairman of the Symposium on Christian Culture, co-sponsored by Rosemont College and Villanova University in the summer of 1959. This symposium brought together for panel discussions of Christian culture, Christopher Dawson and faculty representatives from different colleges and universities in the Eastern part of the United States.

SPECIFIC PROGRAMS FOR THE STUDY
OF CHRISTIAN CULTURE

SECTION I

In discussing the proposals which Christopher Dawson advances in the present volume for the study of Christian culture, one of the first matters to be considered is how these proposals might be realized within the actual structure of the college or university curriculum. Professor Dawson's own consideration of this problem is given in the following passage from Chapter XI above:

... It is a question of adjustment which must be solved in different ways in different places according to the needs and opportunities of the particular society and institution.

The situation is not unlike that which the non-Catholic colleges have to face in so far as they try to combine a general study of "Western civilization" with the special studies of the particular student, and the same methods can be applied to the study of Christian culture. Moreover it might be possible to give different courses in Christian culture appropriate to the different studies being taken; thus the course could be orientated towards either literature, history, art, the classics, philosophy or theology or education. Alternatively, we can conceive the study of Christian culture as the province of a special institute on the graduate level. Or it might be offered as a field of concentration to the student in his later years of undergraduate study. In this case, it could be co-ordinated with the student's vocational preparation so as to lead, for example, to teaching on the secondary or collegiate level or to postgraduate studies in law.[1]

Based upon Professor Dawson's suggestions which we have just quoted and looking to the programs of general or liberal education already in existence in American colleges and universities,[2] there are at least five different ways in which a formal program in Christian culture studies might be inaugurated (as distinguished from the informal leavening of existing courses by insights and ideas related to the Christian culture concept):

1. A program of Graduate Study (which might be related to a graduate institute).
2. An Upper Division field of concentration.
3. A Lower Division fulfillment of liberal education requirements.
4. A program spanning the Lower and Upper Divisions of the college.
5. An Honors program.

What would be the actual courses that might be given on each of these five levels for incorporation of Christian culture study into the college or university? Accepting the fact that all blueprints of this nature are subject to variation and revision in terms of the actual circumstances and resources of the college

[1] Attention should be called to the fact that, although Professor Dawson has had Catholic education primarily in mind in his advocacy of Christian culture studies, he also hopes to encourage consideration of his proposals in terms of the goals sought by the non-Catholic colleges and universities, whether these be denominational or non-sectarian. Consequently, most of the courses mentioned in this Note are intended for use, not only by Catholic colleges, but by any college program of liberal studies which recognizes the affinity between Christianity and the Western humanist tradition.

[2] See *General Education: an Account and an Appraisal,* by Lewis Mayhew (New York, Harper, 1960) for a description of these programs.

or university, I nevertheless think it will serve to stimulate thought upon the matter and serve as a basis for later action, if certain definite course offerings are specifically set down and described.[1] Some of these courses are already in existence and have been given on one or more occasions; others are simply blueprints which need to be subjected to experiment and trial. Others again have been given, but on a more condensed basis than is here suggested. All of them, however, are derived from the ideas concerning the relationship between Christianity and culture which Christopher Dawson discusses in the present volume, and which indeed have formed the integrating principle of his work over the last thirty-five years.[2]

THE PROGRAM OF GRADUATE STUDY

This program, which might possibly be administered through a graduate institute of Christian culture, would offer courses which would be counted for graduate credit towards the master's or the doctor's degree in any one of a number of disciplines, either of the humanities or the social sciences or in philosophical or theological studies. The custom which prevails at most graduate schools of allowing or encouraging the graduate student to take one or more minors to support his major field of study might here be employed to permit the student to add a certain number of Christian culture courses in

[1] While recognizing the validity of Professor Dawson's observation that "the planning of the curriculum must be a co-operative task," with "the whole subject being discussed by a committee of experts," I believe that, in order to arrive at that stage, a preliminary statement of the different means for realization of Christian culture needs to be provided.

[2] See *The Dynamics of World History* for a compendium of these ideas, and such recent books as *The Movement of World Revolution* and *The Historic Reality of Christian Culture* for their application to the present cultural crisis.

fulfillment of his requirements for a minor. As a means of developing an understanding of the interdisciplinary dimensions of the study of Christian culture, and providing a broader view of its unifying effects, it seems advisable that a student take the Christian culture courses in some discipline not too closely related to that of his major field.

SUGGESTED COURSE OFFERINGS

The Theological Foundations of Christian Culture. A consideration of the relation between theology and Christian culture through the study of such subjects as: the Incarnation as the center of human history; the Church as the extension of the Incarnation in time; the Church as the representative of a specialized historical tradition which it has a mission to renew and transmit; the Augustinian conception of the historical process as developing through the conflict of opposing spiritual forces; the Communion of Saints as a bond of historical continuity between past, present and future generations; the doctrine of the End of History and the Last Things.

The Historical Development of Revelation. A study of the Jewish-Christian tradition, here seen historically and dynamically as the development of the spiritual tradition of the Old and New Testaments, which contain the sacred history of the Peoples of God—the old and the new Israel.

Christian Social Institutions. The Christian family and the Christian state. The Christian tradition of law and the idea of the Law of Nature. The Christian conception of liberty and authority and of personal and corporate rights. The Christian attitude toward wealth and poverty: the service of the poor and the institutions arising from it. Christian education and educational institutions. The comparative study of Christian institutions as developed by the different national cultures.

The Study of Christian Thought. Hellenism and the Christian tradition: the Platonism of the Greek Fathers; the Augustinian tradition. St. Thomas and the *Philosophia Perennis.* Scholasticism and the birth of Western science. Humanism and Christian philosophy. The relation of modern Western philosophies to the Christian tradition. Christian rationalism and the rationalism of the Enlightenment. Christian idealism and the idealism of the Romantic philosophers. Christianity and technology.

Christianity and Comparative Culture. The chief approaches which anthropology affords for the study of a culture and its institutions and values. The extension of these approaches to the study of civilizations, with particular reference to the comparative study of the civilization of Christendom and that of one of the Oriental religion cultures.

Christianity and the Open Society. The meaning of such terms as "open" and "closed" in relation to society and culture, and the questions raised concerning these issues by Bergson and Toynbee. A consideration of the critiques of modern mass culture by sociologists and humanists in their relation to the issue of an open society. Christianity and the transcendence of religious values and their effect upon society and culture. A consideration of the relevance of the Christian conception of culture to the modern criticisms of mass society.

Christianity and Church-State Relationships. A study of the changing relationship between Church and State in the historical development of Christian culture: attitudes concerning Church and State in the early Church, in the Byzantine empire, in medieval Europe after Gregory VII, and the different conceptions and practices in this matter of post-Reformation Catholicism, Lutheranism, Calvinism, Anglicanism, and the sects. A consideration of the different ways in which the French Revolution and the American Constitution have affected the development of Church-State relationships.

The Missionary Expansion of Christianity. A study of the expansion of Christianity throughout the centuries with reference to those factors which have helped or hindered its spread to new peoples. Comparison of the main features of the expansion of Catholicism in the sixteenth and seventeenth centuries with the missionary activities of Protestantism in the nineteenth and twentieth centuries.

The Protestant Sects and Their Influence upon Culture. A consideration of the Protestant sects as different ways of religious life, and their sociological analogy to the religious Orders in Catholic Christendom. The interaction between the ideals of the sects and the cultural forces with which they came into contact, and the effects of this on the formation of social ideals and patterns in England and America. A comparison of the relation of the sects to cultural development in Russia with that in England and the United States.

Prophecy and Culture Change. A consideration of the nature of prophetic testimony and its significance for the conditions of modern culture. A study of the effect upon Western culture of such prophetic figures as St. Augustine, St. Odo of Cluny, Gregory VII, St. Bernard, Martin Luther, George Fox, John Wesley, Kierkegaard, Newman, and in the secular sphere, Rousseau and Karl Marx.

Christianity and the Development of Western Science. The character of Western culture, and the influence of Christianity and of science upon its formation. The significance of the technological development of science in Western culture and its relation to the ethos of Western Christianity. A study of the interaction between scientific and Christian attitudes in certain key figures in the history of scientific development: Roger Bacon, Francis Bacon, Copernicus, Galileo, Descartes, Newton, Locke, etc.

Christianity and Conceptions of World History. A discussion of the different views of world history held by certain key figures from the Enlightenment to the present and their evaluation and critique in terms of the Christian understanding of history. The Rationalist and the Romantic conceptions of history. Hegel, Marx, Burckhardt, Nietzsche, Spengler and Toynbee are among those studied in the development of historical consciousness since the eighteenth century. A consideration of Dawson's view of the development of world history as an example of the interaction between the Christian conception of history and the fruits of modern historical knowledge.

The Prophets of Literature and the Culture of Christendom. An examination of the developing social crisis and the separation of religion from culture since the French Revolution, as seen in the thought of such men as Novalis, de Maistre, Lamennais, Kierkegaard, Dostoievski, Newman, Ruskin, Carlyle, Arnold, Pater, Henry Adams, Santayana. A study of their attitudes toward the Christian culture of the past in relation to the cultural situation of their own time.

The Six Ages of Christian Culture. A consideration of the main themes that give each age its specific character and cultural outlook. The permanent contribution of each age to the subsequent development of Christian culture. The pattern of historical development followed by each age in its rise and decline.

For a more intensive examination of the historical development of Christian culture, courses might be provided on one or several of the six periods of its history:

The Early Church and the Rise of Christian Culture
Byzantine Culture and the Age of the Fathers
The Formation of Western Christendom
Medieval Christendom and the Gothic Culture
Divided Christendom and the European National Cultures
Secularized Christendom and the Age of Revolution

The Ecumenical Councils and the Development of Doctrine. The conception of doctrinal development, with special reference to its analysis by Cardinal Newman. The Ecumenical Councils as the focus for the encounter of certain historical and cultural factors which require the response of an explication of doctrine and thus set the conditions for doctrinal development. The problems faced by certain selected councils as examples of the process by which the development of doctrine takes place. A consideration of the interaction between transcendental and historical factors in the development of the Church's teaching.

The Problem of Christian Unity. A consideration of the meaning of the unity of the Church and the different interpretations placed upon it. Problems to Christian unity resulting from the historical heritage of divided Christendom. The impact of developments in secular history upon the division of Christendom, both before and after the French Revolution. The development of the ecumenical movement within Protestantism and its influence upon Protestant attitudes toward the Catholic Church and its tradition.

THE UPPER DIVISION FIELD OF CONCENTRATION

This program would constitute a major field of study for the student in his junior and senior years. It would be advisable to arrange the Christian culture studies in such a way that the student in the program would pursue a double major: one in a regularly established discipline, such as History, English, Foreign Languages, Education, Sociology, Philosophy, etc., and one in the interdepartmental discipline of Christian culture.

As an example of the Upper Division field of concentration we give below the courses developed at St. Mary's College, Notre Dame, Indiana, under the chairmanship of Dr. Bruno Schlesinger. This program has been in successful operation for the past five years. The core courses are those in Christianity and Culture (4 terms) and in the Colloquia (4 terms). The other four courses constitute exploration in depth of particular subjects from a Christian culture standpoint. Depending on the resources of the particular college or university, one or more of the courses mentioned above as part of a graduate program might be either added to this group of courses or used in place of some of them.

COURSES OF STUDY

Christianity and Culture I: The Making of Europe. The formation of Christian culture in both East and West down to the eleventh century. 3 sem. hrs.

Christianity and Culture II: Medieval Christendom. The maturity of Christendom in the age of St. Thomas and Dante and the growth of Gothic culture to the fifteenth century. 3 sem. hrs.

Christianity and Culture III: The Age of Religious Division. The expansion and disintegration of Christendom to the eighteenth century; Humanism, Baroque Culture, the Enlightenment. 3 sem. hrs.

Christianity and Culture IV: The Age of Revolutions and World Wars. World ascendancy of secularized Western Culture; internal and external forces of disintegration. Nationalism, Communism and the Totalitarian State. 3 sem. hrs.

Colloquium I: Christian Classics. The study and discussion of works, such as St. Augustine's *Confessions* and *The City of God;* the Rule of St. Benedict; Bede's *Ecclesiastical History; The Song of Roland;* the Legends and Lauds of St. Francis of Assisi; Latin Hymns and Sequences; and Byzantine Art. 2 sem. hrs.

Colloquium II: Christian Classics. The study and discussion of works, such as St. Thomas Aquinas' *On Kingship,* Joinville's *Life of St. Louis,* Dante's *Divine Comedy,* Langland's *Piers Plowman,* Chaucer's *Canterbury Tales; Revelations of Divine Love,* by St. Juliana of Norwich; the Trial of Joan of Arc; *Everyman;* Romanesque and Gothic Art. 2 sem. hrs.

Colloquium III: Significant Books of Divided Christendom. The study and discussion of works, such as Erasmus' *Colloquies,* St. Thomas More's *Utopia,* St. Teresa's *Life,* Hooker's *Laws of Ecclesiastical Polity;* Poems by Donne, Herbert, Crashaw and Vaughan; Milton's *Paradise Lost,* Calderon's *Life is a Dream,* Pascal's *Pensées,* Fénelon's *Letters,* Swift's *Argument against*

Abolishing Christianity, Pope's *Essay on Man;* Renaissance and Baroque Art.

Colloquium IV: Significant Books of Divided Christendom. Burke's *Reflections on the Revolution in France*, Goethe's *Faust* (Part One), Newman's *Idea of a University*, Orestes Brownson's *Essays*, Hawthorne's *The Scarlet Letter*, Kierkegaard's *Fear and Trembling*, Marx and Engels' *The Communist Manifesto*, Dostoievski's *The Possessed*, Ibsen's *The Master Builder*, G. M. Hopkins' *Poems*, Bloy's *Pilgrim of the Absolute*, Chesterton's Essays, Mauriac's *Vipers' Tangle*, T. S. Eliot's *Murder in the Cathedral;* Nineteenth Century Art and Contemporary Art.

Early Christian Writers. An introduction to the writings of St. Clement of Rome, St. Ignatius of Antioch, Tertullian, Origen, St. Athanasius, St. Jerome and St. John Chrysostom. 2 sem. hrs.

History of Christian Philosophy. An introduction to the history of philosophical ideas in the Middle Ages from St. Augustine to William of Ockham. 2 sem. hrs.

Church, State and Society. An examination of the impact of Christianity upon such social institutions as the family, slavery, property, the state, and an introduction to the enduring problems raised by the claims of Church and State. 2 sem. hrs.

Christianity and American Culture. A study of the roots of American culture in Christianity and in the Enlightenment from colonial times to the present, with special emphasis upon the age of Jefferson and the age of Emerson. 2 sem. hrs.

Beginning with the academic year 1960–61 there has been added to the curriculum a course of lectures on the Oriental religion cultures, given in a two-year cycle by visiting lecturers from the University of Chicago and other outside sources.

The first year's lectures deal with Chinese and Islamic cultures, the second year with the religion cultures deriving their inspiration from Indian sources, such as Hinduism and Buddhism.[1]

THE LOWER DIVISION PROGRAM IN LIBERAL EDUCATION

The Lower Division program is set up to provide the student with a general education in the freshman and sophomore years, before he enters upon his specialized studies in the later years of college. This type of program is the one most commonly used in American colleges and universities for the presentation of the Western cultural heritage; the Columbia University curriculum in Contemporary Civilization is possibly the earliest and best-known of these programs.

For the adequate study of Christian culture, a Lower Division program should involve four semesters of cultural history. Their presentation would be primarily the responsibility of the department of History, but it would also enlist the aid, through consultation and special lectures, of members of other departments such as Sociology, Literature, Foreign Languages, Classics, Art, Music, etc. Since the six periods of Christian culture delineated by Mr. Dawson would have to be presented in four semesters, it would require a shorter treatment of some periods compared with others. It is possible that it might be found preferable to handle the first two periods of Christian culture during the first semester, under the general heading Christianity and the Ancient World, and the two medieval periods in the second semester (Christianity and the Medieval World), which would then allow a semester for each of the two periods—that of Divided Christendom, 1500–1750, and

[1] For another account of the Saint Mary's College program, see the article by Mr. John P. Gleason in Section II of this Appendix.

that of the Age of Revolution, 1750 to the present—dealing with Christianity in the modern world. However, should there be greater interest and more faculty resources available for the ancient and medieval sequences, then it might well be preferable to provide the more detailed treatment in the opposite direction from the emphasis on the modern periods.

In addition to the four periods of cultural history, a two-semester course in English Literature in the sophomore year could be established so as to co-ordinate with study of Christian culture since the Renaissance being given by the History department during this same sophomore year. This would allow both Literature and History to benefit from the sharper focus in clarity of perception and understanding which each subject would gain from the reinforcement provided by the other.

Moreover, as forming part of the reading list for freshman students in English, it might be possible to introduce the students to certain works which would enable them to grasp the nature of Christian culture and its achievements. Such works might well take on a deeper significance for the student because of his concomitant study of the historical development of Christian culture in his history courses of that year. As an illustration of the type of reading that might be done along this line, we would suggest the following specific examples. (The faculty of each particular college would best be able to judge which and how many of these works might be found suitable for the level of the student at their institution. Of course if this Lower Division program is made part of an Honors program, the quality of work expected of the student would be correspondingly higher.)

Dawson, "St. Augustine and His Age" (in *A Monument to St. Augustine*, ed. by Martin D'Arcy); Chesterton, *The Ballad of the White Horse;* T. S. Eliot, *Murder in the Cathedral; The Little Flowers of St. Francis;* Dante, *The Divine Comedy* (the Inferno and the last ten cantos of the Paradiso); Undset, *The Bridal Wreath* (the first volume of the Kristin Lavransdatter trilogy) or *The Axe* (the first volume of the Master of Hestviken tetralogy); H. F. M. Prescott, *The Man on a Donkey;* Péguy, *Men and Saints;* Chesterton, *Orthodoxy;* Greene, *The Power and the Glory;* Koestler, *Darkness at Noon;* Dawson, *The Movement of World Revolution.*

Finally, it would help the student to realize the historical source of the Christian cultural tradition and how its roots extend far back into ancient history if the freshman course in Religion were so arranged as to provide a view of the historical development of Revelation, through the successive stages of Jewish history to its eventual culmination in the Gospel and the new religious community of the Church. Of the first part of this program, the study of the Old Testament, Christopher Dawson has written: "The study of the Old Testament is especially valuable from the cultural angle, and it gives one a starting point on the Christian view of history, which is unintelligible without a good knowledge of the Old Testament. . . . If we wish to find the roots of the Christian interpretation of history, we must go back behind the Fathers, behind the New Testament, behind even the Hebrew prophets to the very foundation of the religion of Israel."[1]

If the biblical-historical approach to the Religion program were carried over into the second year, the first term might deal with the establishment of the first Christian communities

---

[1] The first part of this passage is from a letter addressed by Professor Dawson to the present writer; the second is from *The Dynamics of World History,* p. 252.

and the development of Christian teaching as seen in the Acts of the Apostles and in selections from St. Paul's Epistles; while the second term might study the liturgy as manifesting the continuity between the Old and New Testaments and exhibiting the full historical scope of the Christian mystery of man's redemption. It would thus serve as a recapitulation of the sacred history which had been studied in the preceding terms and would make the student aware of the form in which that history was being communicated to future generations of Christians to the end of time.

SUGGESTED COURSE OFFERINGS

THEOLOGY COURSES

Israel and the Scriptures. A study of the successive stages of revelation—Mosaic, Prophetic and Christian—each of these stages involving not simply a question of new truths, but of events through which the truths are revealed. In the first term's work the study of this development in the Old Testament, the prehistory of the Incarnation, as seen in such events as the calling of Abraham, the covenant between God and Israel at Sinai, the history of the Chosen People, and the successive revelations by the Prophets as to the nature of the Kingdom of God.

The Gospel and the Kingdom. In this second term's work, a study of the Incarnation as the fruit of history, the dispensation of the fullness of time. The Gospel as the fulfillment of the heritage of Jewish prophecy concerning the Messiah and the restoration of Israel, but also the beginning of a new world order which would renew all things through the action of the historical person of Jesus. An examination of the twofold character of the Kingdom portrayed in the Gospel: internal and spiritual, a leaven in the heart of man which is in the process of creating a new humanity; and external and cosmic, the universal Kingdom of the Son of Man, the consummation of human history, which is as yet present only in embryo in the womb of the old order.

The Apostolic Church. The establishment and spread of the early Christian communities in the Graeco-Roman world, as narrated in the Acts of the Apostles. The development of the Christian Revelation in St. Paul's Epistles, and the relation of this development to the challenges presented to St. Paul in his apostolate to the Gentiles. The principal themes of St. Paul's teaching.

The Liturgy and Sacred History. The liturgy as the recapitulation of the mystery of Divine Providence in bringing to fulfillment the Incarnation and Redemption in "the fullness of time." A study of the liturgy as based on a sacred history and presenting this in an historical cycle in which the whole story of human creation and redemption is progressively unfolded, as the revelation of the Divine purpose on earth and in time. The close inner relation and counterpoint between the movement in the Old Testament and in the New, as seen especially in the Advent and Paschal liturgy.

Each of these courses might be either two or three semester hours.

CULTURAL HISTORY

Christianity and the Ancient World. A study of the process of interpenetration between the Christian tradition and Gentile culture in the early Christian Church (before Constantine) and in the Byzantine Empire down to the opening of the seventh century. The interaction between Hebraic, Oriental, Greek and Roman cultural elements in the first six centuries of the Christian era, and the manner in which Christianity served to integrate these elements in a new religious culture. A comparison and contrast of the main features of Christian culture during the first three centuries of Primitive Christianity with that of Patristic Christianity in the following period, which saw the conversion of the Roman-Hellenistic world and the rise of Byzantine culture.

Christianity and the Medieval World. A study of the interpenetration of barbarian culture by the higher cultural tradition which Christianity brought to Northern Europe from the Mediterranean world. The mutual influences by which the barbarians were Christianized and Christian culture incorporated certain barbarian institutions and social patterns in its new cultural synthesis. A comparison of the key features and social organs of Christian society during two successive periods or phases of the history of the medieval world: the predominantly rural culture of Northern Europe during the first five centuries of Christianization (the period of the Formation of Western Christendom), and the mixed feudal and urban culture which resulted from the renewed contact of medieval Europe with Greek learning in the eleventh and the twelfth centuries, leading to the flowering of Gothic culture in the second half of the medieval millennium.

Christianity and the Modern World. An examination of the changes in Christian culture brought about by two different developments in two successive periods of modern history: (1) the expansion of Christian culture and the division of

Christendom in the period from the Renaissance to the Enlightenment; (2) the Revolution and its social and political consequences in the period from the eighteenth to the twentieth centuries. A comparison of the new forms of Christian culture developed in Protestant and Catholic Europe in response to the challenge of the Renaissance and the Reformation with the impact of the European revolution upon these forms in the last century and a half.

Note: If the first two sequences in the cultural history are each given in one semester, so that two semesters are allowed for the third member of the sequence, Christianity and the Modern World, then it is suggested that some provision might be made for giving to cultural history in the freshman year four semester hours each term instead of three. This would permit more adequate attention to be given to each of the first two sequences and would afford opportunity for some attention to the literature in which the process of cultural transformation could be seen taking place. Thus, in the first of these sequences, Christianity and the Ancient World, an extra semester hour each week should make it easier for the student to learn some of the representative ideas of Plato, Cicero and Marcus Aurelius, in selected passages from their work, and see their relationship to the thought of the first Christian centuries. (Ernest Barker's volume, *From Alexander to Constantine* [Oxford, 1956], is most helpful for a study of certain aspects of this development, although it stops short of the great age of the Fathers of the Church.) Thus, for example, ideas concerning the soul and its future might be compared in Plato (see the Livingstone edited volume of Plato in the World's Classics series) with those in Tertullian's *Testimony of the Soul;* or the relation between man and God in Marcus Aurelius's *Medi-*

tations with the new conception to be found in St. Augustine's *Confessions*. And there are many other examples of the way in which the literature of the period illustrates the nature of the social and spiritual change taking place as Christianity gradually replaces Hellenic philosophy and *paideia* as the accepted religion of the ancient world. (Werner Jaeger's brief volume on *Humanism and Theology* is rich with insights on the change in values which was taking place, although he tends to stress the continuity with the past more than some other writers are likely to do.)

For the course on Christianity and the Medieval World, the student should be expected to read such works (or significant parts thereof) as Bede's *Ecclesiastical History*, Joinville's *Life of St. Louis*, the Franciscan missionary narratives found in *The Mongol Mission* (in The Makers of Christendom series), selections from *Piers Plowman*, and the Prologue to *The Canterbury Tales*. And, if *The Divine Comedy* and *The Little Flowers of St. Francis* are not read as part of the reading list in freshman Literature, then they should certainly be included here.

In addition to this, a certain time should be set aside for the use of either filmstrips or film slides showing the different styles of architecture and sculpture of the different periods of the Christian cultural development, as well as how styles were affected by variations from one country to another (e.g., differences between Roman basilicas and Byzantine churches, between Romanesque and Gothic, Renaissance and colonial Baroque, colonial styles in Mexico and in the Spanish missions contrasted with those of colonial New England, modern church architecture in Europe and in the United States, etc.).

Filmstrips or film slides (in color) should also be used to

show the different schools and masters of painting from the Byzantine era down to the present, with special reference to their reflection of cultural values and attitudes and the influence of both Christianity and secular cultural currents upon them.[1]

For these reasons, an additional hour for the course each of the two semesters of the freshman year would be highly desirable if an adequate account is to be given of the first four periods of Christian culture (that is, on the premise that these will be covered in the first two semesters of the four available in a Lower Division program).

As an example of what is available in filmstrips and film slides from just one publisher, the following items from the Herbert E. Budek Company of Hackensack, N.J., may be cited: *In color:* Ten sets of Italian paintings of different schools, 35 to 40 frames each; six sets of Flemish paintings of different schools, 30 to 35 frames each; six sets of Mosaics and Frescoes in Italian Church Buildings, 35 frames each; one set on the Mission Churches of New Mexico, 32 frames; two sets on the paintings of Rouault, 33 frames each. *In black and white:* The History of Western Art, comprising 30 sets of filmstrips and film slides, including such subjects as: (1) Greek Art, 2 sets of 40 frames each; (2) Early Christian, Byzantine and Migration Art, one set of 40 frames; (3) Architecture and Sculpture of the Early and the Late Middle Ages, 2 sets of 40 frames each; (4) Illuminated Manuscripts, one set of 40 frames; (5) Archi-

[1] For a general survey of material available for these purposes, see Edgar Dale's *Audio-Visual Methods in Teaching* (1954), and more specific guides such as Milton Brooke and Henry J. Dubester's *Guide to Color Prints* (1953), William Chapman's *Films on Art* (1952), and UNESCO's *Films on Art* (1951). (These are cited by Patrick D. Hazard in his article in *Contemporary Literary Scholarship* [1958], ed. by L. Leary.)

tecture, Sculpture, and Painting of the Renaissance, 3 sets of 40 frames each; (6) Architecture, Sculpture and Painting of the Baroque, 2 sets of 40 frames each; (7) The Cathedrals at Reims and Chartres, 2 sets of 40 frames each; (8) Architectural Styles: Romanesque, Gothic, Renaissance, Baroque, 1 set of 60 frames; (9) Impressionism and The Art of the Twentieth Century, 2 sets of 35 frames each. In addition, there are two other black and white series available: twelve sets dealing with the History of American Art, from 1600 to 1930; and five sets dealing with Italian Architecture, from the Florentine Renaissance to the eighteenth century.

LITERATURE COURSES— SOPHOMORE YEAR

Literature and the Baroque Culture. A reading and discussion of certain selected works from the Renaissance to the eighteenth century. The focus will be on the coexistence of two contrasting influences on the culture of this period: the luxuriance and fantasy and passion of the Baroque spirit, and the sobriety and dedication and moral earnestness of the Protestant ethos, and their eventual replacement by the rationalism of the Enlightenment. Representative works that might be chosen for study include: Marlowe's *Dr. Faustus*, Shakespeare's *Macbeth* or *Antony and Cleopatra*; John Donne: selected sermons and poems; Cervantes' *Don Quixote* (Part One), Pascal's *Pensées*, Milton's *Paradise Lost* (first four books) and *Samson Agonistes*; Camoens' *Lusiads*, Bunyan's *Pilgrim's Progress*, Defoe's *Robinson Crusoe*; Jonathan Edwards: selections; Dryden's *The Hind and the Panther*, Pope's *Essay on Man*.

Literature and Modern Culture. A reading and discussion of selected works which represent the main streams of cultural development since the eighteenth century. A focus for most of the works selected should be found in one or another of three principal features of the cultural situation of this period: (1) the revolutionary attitude toward the established order of thought and social organization, which resulted from the Enlightenment and the French Revolution and produced reactions as various as Novalis' *Europe or Christendom*, Marx's *The Communist Manifesto*, and Nietzsche's *The Antichrist;* (2) the increasing isolation of the individual consciousness from the new technical society that was developing in the nineteenth and twentieth centuries: Freud's work (see, for example, *Civilization and Its Discontents*) and the parallel to his thought in modern poetry and fiction suggest possible selections for inclusion under this heading; (3) the effect upon the religious conscience of the growing secularization of society. (For example, Kierkegaard's *Attack upon " Christendom,"* Newman's conflict with the Liberalism of his age, Matthew Arnold's criticism of Philistine values, as also the thought of the other Victorian "prophets," all have their origins in this cultural situation.)

THE PROGRAM SPANNING THE LOWER AND UPPER DIVISION

In this type of program, there would be time to devote one semester to each of the six periods of Christian culture and at the same time provide an exploration of the historical roots of the Christian tradition in the Old and New Testaments. Thus the freshman year would permit the Religion department of the college or university to present two historically oriented courses on the Scriptures, along the lines described for the Lower Division program; and if faculty resources and curricular arrangements permitted, this might be continued into the sophomore year with a study of the Apostolic Church and the Liturgy, also as described above. This second year might be made optional for the student, so that he might choose either this or some other approach to the study of Religion in the denominational college. Thus the courses which could be offered would include (see the titles under the Lower Division program for content and approach):

Freshman Year: Israel and the Scriptures
                      The Gospel and the Kingdom
Sophomore Year: The Apostolic Church
                      The Liturgy and the Christian Mystery

Beginning with the first term of the sophomore year, the student would be introduced to the study of Christian culture in itself, and he would thenceforth take one course in Christian culture (covering each of the six periods) each term until he had concluded his senior year. This would allow for a more leisurely approach to the subject and would give the student an opportunity to engage in more outside reading in connection with the course being taken. For this reason it should be possible to have key works of literature read in connection with the course rather than having them form part of a separate literature course related to Christian culture. However, two supplementary arrangements should be considered as a means of providing the student with a maximum of communication with Christian culture insights and understandings:

1. During the freshman year, as part of his reading list, the student might be required to read a certain number of books related to the historical development of Christian culture, which would at the same time afford him a rewarding esthetic experience. The choice might be made from the following works: T. S. Eliot, *Murder in the Cathedral;* G. K. Chesterton, *The Ballad of the White Horse* or *Orthodoxy* (or both, if the student became interested in Chesterton's thought); Sigrid Undset, *The Bridal Wreath* (first volume of Kristin Lavransdatter) or *The Axe* (first volume of The Master of Hestviken); Péguy, *Men and Saints* (a selection from his prose and poetry); Christopher Dawson, *The Movement of World Revolution.* There are, of course, numerous other volumes which might be used for the purpose in place of those which are here suggested.

2. For those who have found the Christian culture program a means of integration of their college work, there might be offered in the senior year a choice of either one or both of the courses in Literature we have listed above for the Lower Division program (Literature and the Baroque Culture, Literature and Modern Culture), or a course in different conceptions of world history held by key thinkers since the eighteenth century (see in the list of courses under the graduate program the one entitled Christianity and Conceptions of World History). For those electing to take the Literature course(s) in the senior year, a more mature level of work and exploration of underlying ideas might be expected than from sophomore students taking it in the Lower Division program, and it might serve also as a basis for a senior essay.

The courses in cultural history would include the following: *The Ancient World and the Rise of Christian Culture.* An examination of the chief elements in the culture of the ancient world in the first century B.C. A study of the development of the Christian Church and its influence upon culture during the first three centuries. Christianity's gradual penetration of the dominant urban Roman-Hellenistic culture, reaching its full development in the first half of the third century—the age of Clement and Origen in the East and of Tertullian and Cyprian in the West. A consideration of the main influences that moulded Christian culture during this period: the Bible and its tradition, martyrdom and ideals of Christian spirituality, the Christian conception of history, the Church as the new Israel, etc.

Byzantine Culture and the Age of the Fathers. A study of Byzantine culture from the fourth to the sixth centuries as the translation into Christian terms of the Hellenistic culture of the later Roman Empire. The fourth-century Fathers in East and West and the classical age of Christian thought. The Oriental origins of monasticism, its influence on Byzantine culture and its spread to Western Europe. Byzantine culture as the synthesis of Oriental and Hellenic elements. The flowering of Christian art and architecture and liturgical poetry, reaching its climax in the age of Justinian. Imperial patterns of Church-State relations and their effect upon the Oriental peoples of the Empire. Expansion of Christianity in the Orient. The coming of Islam, and its effects.

The Formation of Western Christendom. A study of the transplantation of Christianity from the civilized world of the Mediterranean to the barbarian world of Northern Europe. The change from urban to rural patterns of culture, and the key importance of monasticism in the new culture. The adaptation of barbarian institutions to Christian purposes. The creation of a Christian-barbarian culture through the mutual interpenetration of its two constitutive elements. The cultural achievements and missionary activities of the Celtic and Anglo-Saxon peoples. The Carolingian renaissance and the foundations of later medieval culture. The Viking and Magyar invasions and the conversion of Northern and Eastern Europe.

Medieval Christendom and the Gothic Culture. A study of the development of medieval culture from the eleventh to the fifteenth century. The creative centuries of Gothic culture as resulting from the union of the dynamic force of the monastic reforming movement with the universal spiritual leadership of the Papacy. The decline of medieval culture when the alliance of these two forces was severed early in the fourteenth century. Expressions of the creative unity of medieval culture in such developments as the Crusading movement and the Cistercian reform, the rise of the communes and the creation of the medieval universities, scholastic philosophy and the poetry of Dante, Gothic architecture and art and the establishment of new forms of monasticism in the Franciscan and Dominican Orders. Medieval culture in the fourteenth and fifteenth centuries as gradually disintegrating the imposing synthesis of the classical age, but producing its own specific cultural achievements: the mysticism of the Rhineland and the Low Countries, the scientific movement in the universities, the rise of national states and parliaments, the poetry of Chaucer and Langland, the art of Burgundy and Flanders, and the development of new styles of Gothic architecture for civic and religious purposes.

Divided Christendom and the Expansion of Western Culture. A study of the response of Western Christendom from the sixteenth to the eighteenth century to the challenges presented by the Protestant Reformation, the new lay culture of the Renaissance, the Turkish conquest of Eastern Europe, and the widening of geographical horizons in Asia and the Americas. The emergence of new patterns of religious culture in Protestant and Catholic Europe, the development of a new form of Christian humanist culture and education, the great expansion of missionary activity by Catholic Europe, and the formation of the new Baroque culture through the fusion of the humanist Renaissance with the Catholic Revival. Widespread influence of the Baroque in Europe and the Americas. The transplantation of Christian culture, in both its Catholic and Protestant forms, to the Americas. The rise of modern science and the international channels for its communication. The retreat of the Baroque culture before the rationalist culture of the Enlightenment.

Secularized Christendom and the Age of Revolution. A study of the rise of revolutionary ideologies and new forms of secularized culture in Europe, and their spread to other parts of the world. The effects of this development upon Catholic and Protestant culture areas and the differing character of their response. Topics to be studied will include: The Enlightenment and the European Revolution. The Impact of Liberalism on Protestant and Catholic Europe. The Industrial Revolution and the World Expansion of Western Culture. The Rise of the United States and New Patterns of Church-State Relations. Christian Missionary Expansion in Asia, Africa and Oceania. Nationalism and the Two World Wars. The Rise of Communism and the Totalitarian State. The Scientific Revolution and the Rise of Mass Culture. The Conflict between Christianity and Secularized Culture. Oriental Nationalism and the Shift in the Balance of World Power. Movements toward World Unity and the Ecumenical Problems of Christian Culture.

HONORS PROGRAM

In accordance with current practice in Honors programs now in existence at American colleges and universities, the student should begin this program in the freshman year and have an opportunity to carry it through to its completion in the senior year. A senior essay should be required, based upon work in a seminar course in the senior year, in which the student would attempt to tie together in the perspective of an integrated view of reality the liberal arts studies he had pursued throughout his college curriculum.

The basic courses in cultural history should be given to the student in the freshman and sophomore year along the lines of the Lower Division program—which provides for a consideration of the interaction between Christianity and culture in three different social milieux—the ancient world, the medieval world, and the modern world. Alternatively, it might be thought preferable to have three years allotted to the study of the cultural development, in which case the required courses would end with the junior year and each of the six periods of Christian culture would have one term allotted to its study.

In the junior and senior years, the student should have the opportunity to take courses in two or more subject fields which would provide exploration in depth of some significant area, problem or historical development viewed from the Christian culture standpoint. At least two of these should be in addition to the seminar course upon which the senior essay is based.

Depending upon the faculty resources available for the Honors program at a particular college or university, the following courses might be found suitable for presentation on this Upper Division level.

1. One of the more specific courses we have listed above in the St. Mary's College Upper Division program: e.g., Ancient Christian Writers; Church, State and Society; Christianity and American Culture.

2. In universities with graduate divisions, the graduate courses listed above under the first of the alternatives suggested—the Graduate Program in Christian Culture Study—might be made available to undergraduate Honors students in the junior and senior years.

3. Courses in particular disciplines that show a cultural-historical orientation and involve understandings related to more than one departmental field. Examples of these, which might also be found helpful as the basis for the senior seminar, are as follows:

Greek Religious Thought and Early Christianity. A study of the religious orientation of Hellenic philosophy from the time of Socrates and Plato down to that of Marcus Aurelius and Plotinus, and the relationship of this tradition to the thought of the Fathers of the Church. An examination of the way in which the Hellenic tradition influenced Christian thought and at the same time was transformed into something new in the process of doing so.

Aspects of the History of Science. A study of the characteristics of scientific thought and the cultural factors that affected it in three different periods: the Hellenistic age,

Europe in the thirteenth and fourteenth centuries, and the rise of modern science in the seventeenth century. Through this, an examination of the relationship of science to the Hellenic and Christian traditions.

The Unity of Philosophical Experience. A study of the philosophical challenge confronting the thinkers of three different periods in the development of Western philosophy: the medieval, the Cartesian, and the modern. A consideration of the responses made by the thinkers of each period and how the solutions arrived at in the historical development of each period suggest a certain unity that characterizes man's philosophic quest.

Christianity and the Renaissance. A study of the effects upon the Renaissance conception of man and the world of the converging influences of Christianity and classical humanism, and of how these affected the most characteristic developments of the period. An examination of the equilibrium between the two forces in the ethos of the Baroque culture and literature. Selections from Petrarch, Marsilio Ficino, Pope Pius II, Pico della Mirandola, Leonardo da Vinci, Erasmus, Leonardo Bruni, Thomas More, Cervantes, Campanella, John Donne, etc.

Spiritual Values and Mass Culture. A comparison of the critique of bourgeois culture in the Victorian period with the twentieth-century criticism of mass culture. Selections from Matthew Arnold and T. S. Eliot (both prose and poetry), and from Ruskin, Riesman, MacDonald, Dawson, Fromm.

Psychology and Comparative Culture. A study of the relationship between psychology, religion and culture, as expressed in the thought of certain key thinkers (e.g., Freud, Jung, William James, Max Weber, Erich Fromm, Bergson, Dawson), and as supported by the evidence of historical societies, both primitive and advanced, and of different periods in the development of Western culture.

The Religion Cultures of the Orient. A comparative study of the ethos and effects upon culture of each of the great world religions of the Orient—Confucianism, Hinduism, Buddhism, Islam. The particular values, institutions, and directions of cultural achievement characteristic of the different Oriental religion cultures. Points of similarity and contrast with Christianity, in both its Eastern and Western forms, and its effects upon cultural development.

The following report has been recommended by Dr. Bruno P. Schlesinger, chairman of the Saint Mary's College Program in Christian Culture (at Notre Dame, Indiana), as providing a good account of the workings and outcomes of the Christian Culture curriculum at Saint Mary's. In a letter to the present writer, Dr. Schlesinger remarked that observers have been particularly impressed by the enthusiasm the program has aroused among the students and the motivation it has given them to attend graduate school.

Mr. Gleason has served as lecturer for the course in Christianity and American Culture in the Saint Mary's program and at present is a member of the History department at the University of Notre Dame. The article which follows is a condensed version of one that appeared in the journal *Religious Education*, the July–August 1960 issue. (Another account of the program was contributed by Mr. Gleason to the April 1959 issue of *The Educational Record*.)

A PROGRAM OF CHRISTIAN CULTURE
by John P. Gleason

There have been in recent years a number of attempts to revitalize the teaching of religion. Many of these attempts have employed some variation of the doctrinal approach to religious education. Saint Mary's College of Notre Dame, Indiana, has explored a new and different avenue in its Program for Christian Culture—a program which endeavors to awaken an appreciation of the depth and richness of the Christian religion through an historical examination of the dynamic role Christianity has played in molding the institutions of Western culture and shaping the values of Western man.

The inspiration for this study of Christian culture came from the writings of the distinguished English scholar, Christopher Dawson, now Stillman Professor of Catholic Theological Studies at Harvard University. Mr. Dawson uses the word "culture" in the anthropological sense to mean the total pattern of life and thought in society; Christian culture as he conceives it is the external embodiment of Christianity in social institutions and modes of human thought and behavior. He has consistently held that religion is the vital formative element in any higher culture, and in several of his best-known works he has traced the influence of the Christian religion in the making of Western culture. The educational program he has suggested would examine this interaction of Christianity with other factors in the development of Western civilization, focusing especially upon "a study of the culture process itself from its spiritual and theological roots, through its organic historical growth to its cultural fruits."

The program for Christian Culture was launched at Saint Mary's in the fall of 1956 under the chairmanship of Dr. Bruno P. Schlesinger. Rather than attempting to install Christian Culture studies immediately as a four-year core curriculum, Saint Mary's began by organizing its Program as an elective interdepartmental major, covering the Junior and Senior years.

This method eliminates many organizational difficulties while permitting a validation of the general approach, and likewise insures that the students who choose to enter the Christian Culture Program will be prepared by two years of basic courses in religion, philosophy, literature, and history. Although Christian Culture is a separate department in the College, offering twenty-eight semester hours of classes, it draws upon members of other departments for instruction, and duplication of courses is avoided.

The Program follows the historical-sociological method suggested by Mr. Dawson, and emphasizes particularly the genetic study of institutions and trends of thought. No attempt is made to provide encyclopedic coverage of so vast and complex a subject; instead certain key periods are selected for intensive examination. In the effort to explore the interaction of Christianity with other factors in the development of Western culture, the Program focusses on the common elements in that development rather than trying to trace the separate histories of the individual nations that comprise the Western world.

In the Junior year the student begins her study of Christian civilization with a course entitled *The Making of Europe,* the first of a sequence of four historically-oriented classes which form the core of the Program. This first semester course is devoted to an examination of the formative stages of Christian culture in East and West and its development down to the eleventh century. Throughout the Program an effort has been made to avoid wherever possible the conventional textbook in favor of works of synthesis which rest on a sound basis of critical scholarship.

Four semesters of colloquium sessions are given concomitantly with the four historical courses. In these weekly discussion classes the student becomes acquainted at first hand with many of the major achievements of Christian civilization in the areas of art, literature, spiritual writing, and social thought. Some of the works considered in the first semester are the *Confessions* of St. Augustine and his *City of God*, the Rule of St. Benedict, Bede's *Ecclesiastical History*, and *The Song of Roland*. A specialist in the area of the work under consideration leads the discussion in these colloquia, but the Chairman of the Program is also present and participates in them to insure the preservation of continuity in the series as a whole. Since the colloquia are closely co-ordinated with the historical sequence, the student has a good background for understanding the specific work under discussion, and each work is fixed solidly in its historical context rather than being viewed as an isolated monument divorced from its cultural milieu.

In the second half of the Junior year, the Program takes up the period of the maturity of Christian culture in the course called *Medieval Christendom*. While the historical sequence provides systematic study of the Middle Ages through such books as Cheyney's *Dawn of a New Era*, the colloquia series includes discussion of Joinville's *Life of St. Louis*, and the poetry of Dante, Langland, and Chaucer, as well as the study of examples of Romanesque and Gothic art.

The second year of the Program traces the development of Western civilization from the fifteenth century to the present day in two courses called *The Age of Religious Division* and *The Age of Revolutions and World Wars*. Here the student reads such well-known works as Hazard's *The European Mind*, and the colloquium sessions range from St. Thomas More's *Utopia* and Pascal's *Pensées* in the first semester to Kierkegaard's *Fear and Trembling* and the poetry of T. S. Eliot in the second.

In bringing the study of Christian civilization down to our own times, the Saint Mary's Program seeks to provide a sharper perspective for understanding the contemporary situation and to avoid engendering in the student a romanticized—and escapist—medievalism. Hence the Program for Christian Culture should not be misinterpreted as an evasion of the obligation to come to grips with the twentieth century. It is, rather, an attempt to deepen the student's knowledge of the historical forces that have made the modern world what it is. Nor does it seem likely that the student will adopt a narrow and exclusive view of Christian culture after seeing how the most diverse elements have been interwoven into the Western tradition, and after considering the positive aspects as well as the secularizing effects of post-Renaissance history.

Besides the historical sequence and the colloquium series, the Program provides for each of the four semesters a more intensive course in some especially significant aspect of Western development. The first of these courses, *Early Christian Writers*, is a systematic introduction to the writings of such men as Tertullian, Origen, St. Athanasius, and St. Jerome— men who are usually known to the student only by allusion or footnote citation. A special course in the history of medieval philosophy is given in the second semester of the Program, concurrently with the course *Medieval Christendom*.

The subjects chosen for special study in the second year of the Program indicate the care Saint Mary's has taken to make the study of Christian civilization meaningful to the student in terms of her own experience. The first of these courses is a historical survey of the relations of Church and State, one of the most complex and pressing of contemporary problems, especially in our pluralistic American society. In the fourth and final semester a course called *Christianity and American Culture* focusses specifically on the interaction of religious influences with other forces in the development of the tradition which is the student's immediate heritage. This course offers a survey of American history, emphasizing close study of Puritanism, the Great Awakening, and the influence of evangelical religion, Benjamin Franklin and the American Enlightenment, Transcendentalism, and the reaction of the churches to industrial society.

The Program for Christian Culture has been immeasurably strengthened and enriched by a lecture series made possible through the generosity of the Lilly Endowment of Indianapolis, Indiana. Assistance from this source has enabled Saint Mary's to institute the Lilly Endowment Lectures, in which distinguished scholars supplement the course work of the Program by their discussion of topics related to the tradition of Christian culture. The quality of the Lilly Endowment series, now in its third year, is suggested by a listing of the participants in the Christian Culture Symposium held in April, 1960. Here Christopher Dawson, Vernon Bourke, Mircea Eliade, Randall Stewart, and Sir Hugh Taylor discussed topics ranging from "History and the Cyclical View of Time" to "Science and Religion."

While Saint Mary's experience with the Program for Christian Culture has been too brief to permit hard and fast conclusions to be drawn, nevertheless certain facts should be noted. For one thing, the Program has attracted students of superior ability. Nearly half of the first graduating class of Christian

Culture majors were honor students. These girls found that the Program not only deepened their knowledge of Western civilization but also increased their appreciation of the Christian religion which has played so important a role in shaping the development of that civilization.

The better students likewise appreciate the relief the Program offers from the standard textbook approach, and they reacted very favorably to the reading of "obscure" and "difficult" authors whom they had previously known only by reputation. They found, often to their surprise, that these authors were not only comprehensible but also rewarding, and that their works frequently had an unexpected contemporary relevance.

In thus awakening the students to the richness of their cultural heritage the Program has achieved one of its purposes. Another encouraging reaction is that many of the students report that the Program assists them in organizing their store of knowledge. They find that information gained in other fields, as well as what they learn in the Christian Culture classes, seems to fit together in a more meaningful pattern and become a part of a comprehensive unity. And although this is rather subjective evidence, it is at least an indication that the study of Christian civilization can perform an integrating function in the undergraduate curriculum.

The organization of the Program for Christian Culture at Saint Mary's is, of course, only a modest experiment, and Saint Mary's does not pretend to have explored all the possibilities of Christopher Dawson's suggestions. But the Program has weathered the difficult years of beginning, and has enjoyed a substantial measure of success. The accomplishments of the

Program's first four years demonstrate that Mr. Dawson's proposals are by no means impracticable, and the religious and educational dividends to be gained from the application of his ideas would seem to warrant further testing and validation of the Christian Culture approach.